HOME AND CHURCH BIBLE STUDY

COMMENTARIES FROM THE

BOOKS OF

GALATIANS

EPHESIANS &

PHILIPPIANS

BY

LARRY D. ALEXANDER

Copyright © 2013 by Larry D. Alexander

All rights reserved. Printed in the U.S.A.

No part of this book may be reproduced

for any purpose except for brief excerpts

regarding reviews or articles by magazines,

newspapers or broadcast, and, use in churches

for Sunday school, bible study, etc.

without the express written consent of the publisher.

Larry D. Alexander

214-649-7671

Larrydalexander01@att.net

Cover designed by

Larry D. Alexander

CONTENTS

PAUL'S LETTER TO THE GALATIANS

ABOUT THE AUTHOR	I
HOW WE GOT OUR BIBLE	II-IV
INTRODUCTION TO THE BOOK OF GALATIANS	V-VII

CHAPTER ONE:
THERE'S ONLY ONE GOOD NEWS	1
PAUL'S MESSAGE COMES FROM CHRIST	2

CHAPTER TWO:
THE APOSTLES ACCEPT PAUL	5
PAUL CONFRONTS PETER	7

CHAPTER THREE:
THE LAW AND FAITH IN CHRIST	10
THE LAW AND GOD'S PROMISES	12

CHAPTER FOUR:
GOD'S CHILDREN THROUGH FAITH	16
PAUL'S CONCERN FOR THE GALATIANS	17
THE TWO CHILDREN OF ABRAHAM	20

CHAPTER FIVE:
FREEDOM IN CHRIST	23
LIVING BY THE SPIRIT'S POWER	25

CHAPTER SIX:
WE REAP WHAT WE SOW	30
PAUL'S FINAL ADVICE TO THE GALATIANS	32

CONTENTS

PAUL'S LETTER TO THE EPHESIANS

INTRODUCTION ---- 35

CHAPTER ONE:

SPIRITUAL BLESSINGS ---- 36

PAUL'S PRAYER FOR SPIRITUAL WISDOM ---- 38

CHAPTER TWO:

WE ARE MADE ALIVE WITH CHRIST ---- 41

JEWS AND GENTILES ARE ONE IN JESUS CHRIST ---- 43

CHAPTER THREE:

GOD'S SECRET PLAN REVEALED ---- 46

PAUL'S PRAYER FOR SPIRITUAL EMPOWERING ---- 48

CHAPTER FOUR:

UNITY IN THE BODY ---- 51

LIVING AS CHILDREN IN THE LIGHT ---- 54

CHAPTER FIVE:

LIVING IN THE LIGHT ---- 58

FAMILY MATTERS ---- 63

CHAPTER SIX:

FAMILY MATTERS (continued) ---- 65

SERVANTS AND SUPERIORS ---- 66

CALLED TO STAND FIRM ---- 68

ABOUT THE AUTHOR

Larry D. Alexander is a well-known visual artist, who was called by GOD several years ago to learn, and to teach GOD's holy word. Alexander has been teaching Sunday school and bible studies for the past ten years, and, has an online weekly Sunday school lesson commentary (http://larrydalexander.blogspot.com/index.html) that is based on the "International Sunday School Lesson" curriculum. He is a devout Christian who lives with his wife of 33 years, Patricia, in Texas' Dallas-Fort Worth area. They have four grown children, one son, and three daughters, and, they also have four grand children. Alexander has written several books that teach and train on the Christian faith doctrine of JESUS CHRIST. Among them are the trilogy, *Sunday lessons from the book of the Acts of the Apostles, Sunday school lessons from the Gospel according to John Mark, and Sunday school lessons from the Apostle Paul's letter to the Romans*, which were aimed at helping Christians conform, more fully, to the word of GOD, in their churches, homes, and communities. The trilogy was followed by bible study guides such as "Home Bible Study Commentaries from the Gospel of John", a complete chapter by chapter study guide of the Apostle John's account of JESUS' three-year ministry here on earth, "Home and Church Bible Study Commentaries from the Book of Hebrews", the book of the bible that, perhaps, exalts the deity of CHRIST JESUS more than any other book in scripture, and "Home and Church Bible Study Commentaries from Paul's Letter to the Romans". This, latest book, "Home and Church Bible Study Commentaries from the books of Galatians, Ephesians, and Philippians" is also written to give believers a little more insight into the letters of the Apostle Paul, and the doctrine of Christianity. This study guide is written to promote Christian spiritual growth, as well as to help us to understand JESUS' life and purpose, and our own life and purpose, as HIS followers. This, like all of Alexander's books, serves to help develop understanding, fear, and reverence for the ONLY WISE GOD, WHO is our SAVIOR through JESUS CHRIST WHO sent us the HOLY SPIRIT.

II

HOW WE GOT OUR BIBLE

Much has been written about how GOD inspired men to write the pages of the bible. GOD used about forty men to write the scriptures and some of these authors remain a mystery even today. The writers of the last chapter of Deuteronomy, the book of Job, and many of the Psalms are classic examples of biblical texts with unknown human authors. We do not have a single manuscript in the handwriting of Moses, Isaiah, Paul, or any other original writer. That of course always leads to this eternal question, "How do we know that the bible we have today is the written word of those original writers who were inspired by GOD?

We already know that GOD did not inspire all those who copied, or translated the bible into various versions, as HE did the original writers. It is quite evident to those who study to be scholars, that, while the original writers were guided and kept from making mistakes by the power of GOD, both copyists and translators were not, and, could and did make errors.

Even though we have no part of the bible in the handwriting of the original writers, we do have two kinds of sources from which we can learn what the original writers wrote. These sources are called "manuscripts" and "versions". "Manuscripts" are documents written by hand. In the days before printing was invented, this was the only way of producing books. There are no known bible manuscripts that were written by the original authors available to man today. However, we have many copies of manuscripts that were copied from the original manuscripts, or, copies of them.

"Versions" are translations of a document into a different language. Some of our ancient versions were actually translated from copies of manuscripts older than any we have today. Therefore, they help us to know exactly what the original writers wrote.

The Old Testament books were written in the Hebrew and Aramaic languages between 1400 and 400 B.C. The oldest bible "manuscript" copies we have today were the ones found among the now famous "Dead

III

Sea Scrolls" in 1947 and later. These copies date back to circa 100 B.C. The oldest known "version" of the Old Testament is the Greek version known as the "Septuagint", which was written by seventy Jewish scholars in Alexandria, Egypt in about 250 B.C., from Hebrew manuscript copies older than any we have today.

In the first half of the second century the bible was translated into Syriac, and not much later, into Latin. A more careful Latin version was completed, around 400 B.C., by the famous scholar Jerome called the "Vulgate", which means "common and proper". This version became the official bible of the Roman Catholic Church, and, of Western Europe. Made from very ancient manuscript copies, this book helps us to be sure the bible we have is approximately the same as the original writings.

In 1380 John Wycliffe and his team of scholars translated the bible into "middle English", a blend of "Norman French and Anglo-Saxon languages. This version was translated directly from the Latin Vulgate. In 1525, William Tyndale wrote an English version, of the New Testament. He later translated some of the Old Testament books into English. His version was translated directly from the original Hebrew and Greek manuscript copies. English churchmen angrily opposed Tyndale's version, and they, along with king Henry VIII, decided instead to go with an English version written by Myles Coverdale. Coverdale used the Latin Vulgate and Martin Luther's German version for his translations.

In Geneva, Switzerland, William Wittington and his group of scholars wrote a revised English version that came to be known as the "Geneva Bible" in 1560. Some of the marginal notes in the Geneva bible offended the Bishops of the Church at England, and this led to the writing of the "Bishops Bible" in 1568. Through the remainder of that century, the Bishop's Bible and the Geneva Bible were split among the churchmen in popularity.

In 1604, however, King James I appointed a commission of 54 scholars, led by Robert Barker, to write a new English version of scriptures. They mostly followed the Bishop's Bible, but they also consulted other English translations, along with the German, Greek and Hebrew text, the Syriac, the Septuagint, and several Latin versions. In 1611 they completed the book that went on to become the most printed and used text in the history of the English Language, "The King James Version" of the Bible.

But as the world would have it, all living languages are constantly changing. Many words used in the King James version are now unknown, or obsolete. Some examples are "nessing", "besom", and "wist". Other words have actually changed their meanings. For example "let", in those days, meant "to hinder" (Romans 1:13). Now, however, it means "to permit". The word "conversation", in those days meant "your whole way of living", but today it just means "talk".

Today, just like in the old days, every Christian needs a bible, translated in their modern native tongue, and in this country that means a "New Living Translation" version of the bible. No translation or version has ever been translated without error, and that includes the "King James Version". And the reason that it has never been done is because there has never been a perfect scholar, or perfect man period, except CHRIST JESUS, and HE didn't choose to write one. But most of our available versions are good enough to familiarize us with the word of GOD that has been handed down to us since the foundation of this world. We should trust that GOD is still with us, just as HE was with the original writers. And while we may think or believe that there may be no more inspired writers, I believe more so that GOD still wants us to get to know HIM through HIS word, and the best way we can understand HIS word is in our own modern-day language. So let's just try and retire the King James Version to our library of reference books, where it can serve us in our studies most efficiently. GOD wants us to get to know HIM and just like in all generations before us, HE raises up scholars to interpret HIS word in our own present-day language.

Larry D. Alexander

INTRODUCTION TO THE BOOK OF GALATIANS

Galatia (modern-day Turkey) was located in central Asia Minor. It was bordered by Cappadocia on the east, Asia on the west, Pamphylia and Cilicia on the south, and to the north, by Bithynia and Pontus. It was a part of the great central plateau of Asia Minor which ranged from 2000 to 3000 feet above sea level.

The north side of Galatia consisted of a series of plains with fairly fertile soil, as this area was situated between several hills creating a valley of sorts. However, the greater part of Galatia consisted of barren uplands that were intersected by small streams of water, and had little or no tree life on its vast plains.

Up unto the third century B.C. Galatia was mainly occupied by Gaulish tribes (people of Celtic descent) who had invaded and took possession some 270 years earlier. However, in 64 B.C. it became a "client-state" of the Roman Empire, and later (25 B.C.), it was incorporated totally into the Roman Empire by Caesar Augustus, and that is how we see it in the days of the Apostle Paul, who evangelized and planted a church there in the first century A.D.

Paul's letter to the Galatians has been called "the Magna Charta of Christian Liberty". It has also been labeled "the short version of Romans", and "the cornerstone of the Protestant Reformation". In the early Church, as the great separation was taking place, the book of Galatians helped to clarify the doctrinal differences between "Judaism" and "Christianity". In fact, it constituted the main theme of the preaching of the Protestant Reformers in the first century and beyond.

In the first century, the Apostle Paul was constantly followed around by Judaizers who taught that, in order to become a Christian, one must first, become a Jew, converting to Judaism, and submitting to all Old Testament laws, including circumcision. The book of Galatians was written to serve as a weapon against this "faith/works" idealism. In it, Paul attempts to explain and defend how the mixing of works with faith robs the Gospel of its power in the life of a believer.

Paul believed that no man could ever earn the favor of GOD. All he could do was to accept the love offered by GOD, and manifest that acceptance through his faith, and, by his throwing of himself on GOD's mercy.

VI

Paul had already preached to the people of Galatia on his first missionary journey with Barnabas (Acts 13:14-14:23). However, shortly after they left Galatia, a group of Jewish believers arrived and began insisting that the Gentile believers submit to the laws of Moses.

Here in this letter to the Galatians, the Apostle Paul points out how Abraham, who lived more than 400 years before Moses was given the law, was accepted by GOD because of his faith in GOD, before the law ever existed. And so, strict adherence to the law is not necessary for one to become a believer, or to make a believer more perfect. We are saved from eternal damnation by accepting JESUS' payment for our sins on our behalf, nothing more, and nothing less. Through our faith and belief in GOD, we will desire to become obedient to HIS laws. And so, our belief triggers our faith, which triggers our desire to be obedient to GOD. Any other kind of teaching can only be viewed as a simple twisting of truth.

The authenticity of Paul's letter to the Galatians has never seriously been questioned, except by those who question all of the Pauline epistles. The sweeping and sometimes reckless statements contained in this letter, along with other familiar characteristics, leave no doubt it is Paul's writings. Even the awkwardness of its Greek, which contains frequent breaks in construction, and bold ellipsis of thought, seems to indicate and validate the tremendous emotional strain under which Paul often wrote.

Galatians is one of Paul's most commanding letters and its importance to the Christian doctrine far exceeds its size. It also gives us insight regarding Paul's life between his conversion on the Damascus road, and missionary journeys that followed (Galatians 1:11-2:14).

This letter to the Galatians can be divided into three sections, each spanning two chapters. The, first section, chapters 1-2, are, more or less, a defense of Paul's apostleship claim and gospel message, while the middle section, chapters 3-4, are more concerned with the subject of "salvation". And finally, the third section, chapters 5-6, deals with "the consequences of saving faith", which is;

- The freedom to love (5:1-15).
- The production of spiritual fruit in the saved individual by the HOLY SPIRIT (5:16-26).
- The needs of others become important in the life of a saved person (6:1-10).

VII

Paul concludes his letter to the Galatians (6:11-16) with a summation of the main points, and a closing admonition, that, he himself, bears the marks of JESUS, and a blessing, in his own body. And I guess, as professed Christians, we should too.

CHAPTER ONE:

THERE'S ONLY ONE GOOD NEWS

Galatians 1:1-10

1 ⁽¹⁾ Paul, an apostle, (not of men, neither by man, but by JESUS CHRIST, and GOD the FATHER, WHO raised HIM from the dead;)
⁽²⁾ And all the brethren which are with me, unto the churches of Galatia:
⁽³⁾ Grace *be* to you and peace from GOD the FATHER, and *from* our LORD JESUS CHRIST,
⁽⁴⁾ WHO gave HIMSELF for our sins, that HE might deliver us from this present evil world, according to the will of GOD and our FATHER:
⁽⁵⁾ To WHOM *be* glory for ever and ever. Amen.
⁽⁶⁾ I marvel that ye are so soon removed from him that called you into the grace of CHRIST unto another gospel:
⁽⁷⁾ Which is not another; but there be some that trouble you, and would pervert the Gospel of CHRIST.
⁽⁸⁾ But though we, or an angel from heaven, preach any other gospel unto you than that which we have preached unto you, let him be accursed.
⁽⁹⁾ As we said before, so say I now again, If any *man* preach any other gospel unto you than that ye have received, let him be accursed.
⁽¹⁰⁾ For do I now persuade men, or GOD? or do I seek to please men? for if I yet pleased men, I should not be the servant of CHRIST.

COMMENTARY:

The importance of any messenger of GOD is never his or her own status, but rather, it is the importance of the status of the ONE WHO sent them. Here in verse 1 of Paul's letter to the Galatians, he claims the absolute highest status of all when he says that he was sent by CHRIST and GOD the FATHER. This set him apart from all those false apostles who were sent by men, and who dogged him all along his missionary journeys.

Paul was astounded by how soon those he had converted were falling away to a different type of gospel, other than the one he originally preached to them when he first established the church at Galatia on his first missionary trip there, a few years earlier (v.6). The Church was now being influenced by false Jewish teachers who claimed to be presenting the same Gospel that Paul preached, but only, theirs was the complete message. This seemed to insinuate that Paul's message was somewhat lacking in the information that he presented, however, Paul insisted that their message radically changed, and indeed, perverted the message of GOD's grace in the Gospel (v.7).

Paul reacted forcefully to these distortions because he deemed it vital to do so. In verses 8 and 9 we see the word "accursed" being used by Paul. It is from the Greek word "anathema" (uh-NATH-uh-mah) which describes "an eternal damnation, or separation from GOD. Here Paul is saying that if anyone, including himself, or even an angel from Heaven, intentionally distorts the Gospel of CHRIST, that person will suffer eternal damnation in the pits of Hell. True men of GOD seek only to please GOD, they do not strive to "tickle the ears" of men.

PAUL'S MESSAGE COMES FROM CHRIST

Galatians 1:11-24

1 (11) **But I certify you, brethren, that the Gospel which was preached of me is not after man.**
(12) **For I neither received it of man, neither was I taught** *it***, but by the revelation of JESUS CHRIST.**
(13) **For ye have heard of my conversation in time past in the Jews' religion, how that beyond measure I persecuted the church of GOD, and wasted it:**
(14) **And profited in the Jews' religion above many my equals in mine own nation, being more exceedingly zealous of the traditions of my fathers.**
(15) **But when it pleased GOD, WHO separated me from my mother's womb, and called** *me* **by HIS grace,**
(16) **To reveal HIS SON in me, that I might preach HIM among the heathen; immediately I conferred not with flesh and blood:**
(17) **Neither went I up to Jerusalem to them which were apostles before me; but I went into Arabia, and returned again unto Damascus.**

(18) Then after three years I went up to Jerusalem to see Peter, and abode with him fifteen days.
(19) But other of the apostles saw I none, save James the LORD's brother.
(20) Now the things which I write unto you, behold, before GOD, I lie not.
(21) Afterwards I came into the regions of Syria and Cilicia;
(22) And was unknown by face unto the churches of Judaea which were in CHRIST:
(23) But they had heard only, that he which persecuted us in times past now preacheth the faith which once he destroyed.
(24) And they glorified GOD in me.

COMMENTARY:

Paul's letter to the Galatians, like his second letter to the Corinthians, eloquently defends his divine authority as an apostle of CHRIST JESUS. It also gives us a summarized version of the gist of his teachings, and, it contains vivid statements of GOD's "justification by faith", as it erects on that foundation, an excellent defense of "Christian liberties", verses "Jewish legalism".

Paul's authority as an apostle was often called into question by the false teachers who followed him around trying to change the new Christian doctrine into the same old doctrine of Judaism which excluded CHRIST JESUS from its teachings. Paul claimed that the gospel he preached was not based on man's point of view, but rather, it was divinely revealed to him by CHRIST HIMSELF. He says that his message came by a direct revelation from JESUS CHRIST, and no one else (v.12).

Here Paul is relating to us about his personal experiences, before and after, that day on the road to Damascus, when he was converted by JESUS CHRIST (Acts 9:3-31). He now realized that GOD had granted him an "undeserved mercy" and called him, even before he was born. GOD then revealed JESUS to him so that he could preach HIS Gospel to the Gentiles of the world, all the remaining days of his life (Galatians 1:15-16).

Paul says he did not rush to consult with any man regarding his divine calling and these next few verses (16b-22) are very much like my own calling to the teaching ministry a dozen years ago. Even today I'm not known in many Christian Churches, despite the massive amount of bible and Sunday school lesson commentaries I've written during that time. Here in verses 17-24, Paul tells of having spent time in Arabia before returning to Damascus and remaining there for three more years. He then finally went to Jerusalem and was introduced to the church leaders by Barnabas (Acts 9:27). He visited with the Apostle Peter and abided with him for fifteen days. The only other person he met with at that time was James, the half-brother of JESUS. Most of the people in the Church were still afraid of him, and didn't want to have anything to do with him because of his previous reputation of persecuting Christians wherever he went. In fact, Paul ended up having to flee Jerusalem after debating with some of the Greek-speaking Jews who sought to kill him (Acts 9:29). He was rescued by some of the Christians who believed his Damascus Road testimony. They took Paul to Caesarea, and from there, sent him back to his hometown of Tarsus.

Paul did not return to Jerusalem until Barnabas went and got him fourteen years later, and took him, first, to Antioch of Syria, and then, on to Jerusalem to report on the success that they had had there, converting Gentiles to Christianity (Acts 11:25-30). In fact, Antioch is where the term "Christian" was first used to describe the followers of CHRIST (Acts 11:25). Up until time they were widely known as "Adherents of the Way", which meant that they abided closely to the ways that JESUS had taught HIS disciples during HIS three-year teaching and preaching ministry here on earth.

CHAPTER TWO:

(5)

THE APOSTLES ACCEPT PAUL
Galatians 2:1-10

2 **(1)** **Then fourteen years after I went up again to Jerusalem with Barnabas, and took Titus with *me* also.**
(2) And I went up by revelation, and communicated unto them that gospel which I preach among the Gentiles, but privately to them which were of reputation, lest by any means I should run, or had run, in vain.
(3) But neither Titus, who was with me, being a Greek, was compelled to be circumcised:
(4) And that because of false brethren unawares brought in, who came in privily to spy out our liberty which we have in CHRIST JESUS, that they might bring us into bondage:
(5) To whom we gave place by subjection, no, not for an hour; that the truth of the gospel might continue with you.
(6) But of these who seemed to be somewhat, (whatsoever they were, it maketh no matter to me: GOD accepteth no man's person:) for they who seemed *to be somewhat* in conference added nothing to me:
(7) But contrariwise, when they saw that the gospel of the uncircumcision was committed unto me, as *the gospel* of the circumcision *was* unto Peter;
(8) (For HE that wrought effectually in Peter to the apostleship of the circumcision, the same was mighty in me toward the Gentiles;)
(9) And when James, Cephas, and John, who seemed to be pillars, perceived the grace that was given unto me, they gave to me and Barnabas the right hands of fellowship; that we *should go* unto the heathen, and they unto the circumcision.
(10) Only *they would* that we should remember the poor; the same which I also was forward to do.

COMMENTARY:

The Apostle Paul wrote his letter to the Galatians for the benefit of the churches that he founded in the district of Galatia very early on in his ministry (circa A.D. 49-50). He had established Christian churches at that time in Derbe, Lystra, Iconium, and Pisidian Antioch, all located in southern Galatia. It was most likely written shortly after the famous (Acts 15) Jerusalem Council, which released Gentile Christian converts from any responsibility to keep the laws that GOD had given exclusively to Jews, such as, for example, circumcision.

This letter was written to rebuke the "faith/works" doctrine that the followers of Judaism, who trailed Paul from church to church, were trying to indoctrinate into the newly founded Christian churches (Galatians 1:6-10). They were also teaching that one must become a Jew first, by conforming to all Jewish laws, before one could be eligible to become a Christian.

This seemed very logical to some new Christians since JESUS HIMSELF was a Jew, which meant that the roots of Christianity itself, was also Jewish. But Paul strongly objected to this kind of teaching and, here in this letter, he clearly explains why mixing works with faith actually robs the Gospel of CHRIST of its power to transform the lives of the new believers.

In Galatians chapter 2, fourteen years after Paul's first visit with Peter in Jerusalem, he returned there, this time with Barnabas and Titus, after being led to do so by the LORD. He met privately with the leaders of the Church to tell them about what he had been preaching to the Gentiles over the years. He wanted to make sure that they did not disagree with his ministry, and of course, they did not. In fact, they didn't even request that Titus, who was a Gentile, be circumcised, as some of the so-called Christians there were demanding (Vs 1-4). Instead, they welcomed Paul and Barnabas as co-workers, and had nothing further to add to what they had been teaching.

As pillars of the Church, Peter, James (JESUS' brother), and John recognized GOD's calling on Paul, and encouraged him to keep preaching to the Gentiles, while they themselves, would keep preaching to the Jews. They only suggested to Paul, Barnabas, and young Titus, that they always remember to help the poor, something they were already more than willing to do (Vs. 6-10).

Christians always need to know when the Gospel of JESUS CHRIST is being distorted, and the only way to know that is to know what the real Gospel presents through a personal relationship with GOD. One must get into the reading and studying of the Word of GOD for themselves and let the HOLY SPIRIT of GOD guide them into all righteousness and knowledge. We must become so familiar with the truth of the Gospel that when we hear counterfeits teaching, it sticks out like a sore thumb.

PAUL CONFRONTS PETER
Galatians 2:11-21

2 **(11)** But when Peter was come to Antioch, I withstood him to the face, because he was to be blamed.
(12) For before that certain came from James, he did eat with the Gentiles: but when they were come, he withdrew and separated himself, fearing them which were of the circumcision.
(13) And the other Jews dissembled likewise with him; insomuch that Barnabas also was carried away with their dissimulation.
(14) But when I saw that they walked not uprightly according to the truth of the gospel, I said unto Peter before *them* all, If thou, being a Jew, livest after the manner of Gentiles, and not as do the Jews, why compellest thou the Gentiles to live as do the Jews?
(15) We *who are* Jews by nature, and not sinners of the Gentiles,
(16) Knowing that a man is not justified by the works of the law, but by the faith of JESUS CHRIST, even we have believed in JESUS CHRIST, that we might be justified by the faith of CHRIST, and not by the works of the law: for by the works of the law shall no flesh be justified.
(17) But if, while we seek to be justified by CHRIST, we ourselves also are found sinners, *is* therefore CHRIST the minister of sin? GOD forbid.
(18) For if I build again the things which I destroyed, I make myself a transgressor.
(19) For I through the law am dead to the law, that I might live unto GOD.
(20) I am crucified with CHRIST: nevertheless I live; yet not I, but CHRIST liveth in me: and the life which I now live in the flesh I live by the faith of the SON of GOD, WHO loved me, and gave HIMSELF for me.
(21) I do not frustrate the grace of GOD: for if righteousness *come* by the law, then CHRIST is dead in vain.

COMMENTARY:

In those early days in the Christian Church, it became a custom of the congregation to gather together weekly for a common meal that they called "The Agape Feast", or, "Love Feast". This meal was made possible by a pooling together of various dishes that were provided by the church members who could afford it. For many of the poor members, this became the only descent meal that they would get all week. In a very special way, this meal represented a moment of togetherness and fellowshipping for Christians of all races, and on all social, and economic levels.

In Galatians 2:11-12, it was just such an occasion that Paul is speaking of, when he had to confront Peter and Barnabas about their hypocritical behavior and attitude toward Gentile Christians. Here Paul tells of a time when Peter, Barnabas, and some other Jewish Christians, even though they had dined with the Gentile Christians earlier, when their fellow Jewish Christian leaders arrived at the feast, they began to shun the Gentile Christians, for fear of what those fellow Jewish legalists might say about socializing with Gentiles.

This act by Peter, and by Barnabas, who were both leaders in the church, led other Jewish Christians to join them in their hypocrisy. Paul, seeing that Peter and the others were not following the truth of the Gospel of CHRIST, confronted Peter and rebuked him publicly in front of all the others, because he was the "ringleader", and his offense against CHRIST's teachings was committed publicly.

In essence, Peter was guilty of rebuilding the old Jewish system of thinking (Judaism) that they had been trying so desperately to move away from. They were trying to be a light for those who were seeking something to believe in, and the new movement toward CHRIST JESUS was taking root all around the world as they knew it, at that time.

Paul understood early on, that a church will cease to be Christian if it contains class distinctions, or anything else, that was contrary to the actions and attitude of JESUS HIMSELF. In GOD's presence, a man's race is meaningless. He is neither regal, nor less-than, and he is neither rich nor poor, but rather, "he is only a sinner for which CHRIST has died".

All but CHRIST has failed to reach the goal that GOD originally set for us when he made us in HIS OWN "spiritual image", by giving us the attributes of HIS OWN nature. However, through HIS grace and mercy HE has since introduced us to a great and relatively easy way to get back into a relationship of friendship with HIM, whereby HE could adopt any man, woman, or child into the "Family of GOD".

It is the blood of CHRIST that allows us to walk into the store of GOD and pick up a "free" bottle of "Faith". And we can take it home and use it to spray some "Hope" on our unclean mirrors, and for the first time, begin to see ourselves as we really are. And with our newfound "Love", we can turn ourselves around, and begin walking in the "newness of life" that can only be found, in CHRIST JESUS.

That is why Paul says that Faith, Hope, and Love are the three great enduring things, and of the three, Love is the greatest (1 cor. 13:13). When we are seeking something to believe in, we should seek GOD, the FATHER of our LORD and SAVIOR JESUS CHRIST, and GOD promises that if we do, through the power of the HOLY SPIRIT, we will certainly find HIM.

CHAPTER THREE:

(10)

THE LAW AND FAITH IN CHRIST
Galatians 3:1-14

3 ⁽¹⁾ O foolish Galatians, who hath bewitched you, that ye should not obey the truth, before whose eyes JESUS CHRIST hath been evidently set forth, crucified among you?
⁽²⁾ This only would I learn of you, Received ye the SPIRIT by the works of the law, or by the hearing of faith?
⁽³⁾ Are ye so foolish? having begun in the SPIRIT, are ye now made perfect by the flesh?
⁴ Have ye suffered so many things in vain? if *it be* yet in vain.
⁽⁵⁾ HE therefore that ministereth to you the SPIRIT, and worketh miracles among you, *doeth HE it* by the works of the law, or by the hearing of faith?
⁽⁶⁾ Even as Abraham believed GOD, and it was accounted to him for righteousness.
⁽⁷⁾ Know ye therefore that they which are of faith, the same are the children of Abraham.
⁽⁸⁾ And the scripture, foreseeing that GOD would justify the heathen through faith, preached before the gospel unto Abraham, *saying*, In thee shall all nations be blessed.
⁽⁹⁾ So then they which be of faith are blessed with faithful Abraham.
⁽¹⁰⁾ For as many as are of the works of the law are under the curse: for it is written, Cursed *is* every one that continueth not in all things which are written in the book of the law to do them.
⁽¹¹⁾ But that no man is justified by the law in the sight of GOD, *it is* evident: for, The just shall live by faith.
⁽¹²⁾ And the law is not of faith: but, The man that doeth them shall live in them.
⁽¹³⁾ CHRIST hath redeemed us from the curse of the law, being made a curse for us: for it is written, Cursed *is* every one that hangeth on a tree:
⁽¹⁴⁾ That the blessing of Abraham might come on the Gentiles through JESUS CHRIST; that we might receive the promise of the SPIRIT through faith.

In Galatians 3:1, the word Paul uses for "foolish" in the original Greek is "anoetos" (an-o-ay-tos), and it simply means "unintelligent", or "unwise". Here it is used to describe how he saw the people of the Church at Galatia when he first heard how they were falling away from the Gospel, and being duped by smooth-talking preachers with anti-CHRIST agendas. It is a word that challenged the Galatians' power of perception and discernment, as they were obviously missing the true essence of the Good News about CHRIST JESUS.

Since Paul had last spoken with them they had taken on a direction that was contrary to what they had been taught earlier, and were actually violating their initial experience with GOD. After beginning their Christian lives in the SPIRIT, they were now trying to become perfect by their own human effort.

Did they now believe that they were saved by their good works, and by keeping the law, instead of by faith? Who had duped them, Paul was now wondering. Seemingly for the Galatians, they believed faith was good enough to "save", but not good enough to live their everyday lives by (Vs. 1-5).

The false teachers that had infiltrated the early Church had come to the people saying that Paul was not really an Apostle because he was not a member of the original twelve. They also pointed to Paul's years of persecuting the Christian Church, up unto the death of Stephen in Jerusalem (Acts 7:57-60). Plus, Paul also had no official appointment from the head Church at Jerusalem.

Paul's answer to these claims was not in the form of an argument, but rather, he simply issued a statement concerning his Damascus Road experience that was witnessed to, by many who were with him on his journey. Besides, no man can make another man into a minister for GOD anyway, for only GOD can do that. The real test of a true man of GOD is not that he has gone through certain rituals or ceremonies, or seminaries, or, taken certain vows, but rather, it is that he has seen CHRIST for himself in his heart, and has received his orders from GOD to do HIS bidding.

Abraham is the human example to whom the Jews, and the Gentiles, look to, as a sort of prototype of one who had a personal relationship with GOD that was based solely on faith. Faith has to have a critical role in anyone's relationship with GOD, be they Jew or Gentile.

The scriptures had always pointed to a time when GOD would accept the Gentile believer into HIS family, based on faith. GOD's promise to Abraham stated that all nations would be blessed through him. Therefore, everyone who puts their faith in CHRIST JESUS, automatically shares the same blessings that Abraham received, because of his faith (Vs. 6-9).

Paul preached the gospel of the free grace of GOD. He believed with all of his heart, that, there was nothing that a man could do to merit the love of GOD. We, as sinners, can only throw ourselves at the foot of GOD in an act of faith, hoping that HE will show mercy on us when we do. It is only through faith that a righteous person is saved, or can have an eternal life in Heaven with GOD.

In the biblical Greek the word Paul uses in verse 13 for "redeemed" is "exagorazo" (ex-ag-or-ad-zo). It is one of only two times in scripture that this particular word appears. The other is in Galatians 4:5, and, in both places it means "to purchase out of slavery", or "to rescue from loss, and thereby, improve the opportunity of".

JESUS has rescued us from the curse of the law. When HE hung on the cross, HE took the curse of the Law upon HIMSELF and exhausted it. HE redeemed mankind when we couldn't redeem ourselves. Through JESUS' vicarious sacrifice, GOD has blessed all those who believe with the same blessing that HE promised to Abraham. And we can all receive the HOLY SPIRIT through faith, which has nothing to do with how well we obey the Law (Vs 10-14). To be in CHRIST, is to be in the place of ultimate trust.

THE LAW AND GOD'S PROMISES
Galatians 3:15-29

3 (15) Brethren, I speak after the manner of men; Though *it be* but a man's covenant, yet *if it be* confirmed, no man disannulleth, or addeth thereto.
(16) Now to Abraham and his seed were the promises made. He saith not, And to seeds, as of many; but as of one, And to thy seed, which is CHRIST.
(17) And this I say, *that* the covenant, that was confirmed before of GOD in CHRIST, the law, which was four hundred and thirty years after, cannot disannul, that it should make the promise of none effect.

(18) For if the inheritance *be* of the law, *it is* no more of promise: but GOD gave *it* to Abraham by promise.

(19) Wherefore then *serveth* the law? It was added because of transgressions, till the SEED should come to whom the promise was made; *and it was* ordained by angels in the hand of a mediator.

(20) Now a mediator is not *a mediator* of one, but GOD is one.

(21) *Is* the law then against the promises of GOD? GOD forbid: for if there had been a law given which could have given life, verily righteousness should have been by the law.

(22) But the scripture hath concluded all under sin, that the promise by faith of JESUS CHRIST might be given to them that believe.

(23) But before faith came, we were kept under the law, shut up unto the faith which should afterwards be revealed.

(24) Wherefore the law was our schoolmaster *to bring us* unto CHRIST, that we might be justified by faith.

(25) But after that faith is come, we are no longer under a schoolmaster.

(26) For ye are all the children of GOD by faith in CHRIST JESUS.

(27) For as many of you as have been baptized into CHRIST have put on CHRIST.

(28) There is neither Jew nor Greek, there is neither bond nor free, there is neither male nor female: for ye are all one in CHRIST JESUS.

(29) And if ye *be* CHRIST's, then are ye Abraham's seed, and heirs according to the promise.

COMMENTARY:

JESUS CHRIST is the one person in whom GOD's covenant with Abraham was consummated. GOD told Abraham in Genesis 17:7-8 that "HE would establish HIS covenant between HIMSELF, Abraham, and his SEED" (seed being singular, not plural). Therefore, this "Abrahamic Covenant" is not consummated in a group of people (the Jews), who were descendants of Abraham, but rather, it was promised to CHRIST, WHO was GOD's OWN SEED, through the genealogical line of Abraham.

In Galatians 3, taking up at verse 15, the Apostle Paul calls on his own Rabbinic training to get his point across to the Christian Church at Galatia. Jewish rabbis were proud of how they could base their arguments on the use of a single word, in this case "seed". Part of a Rabbis training was in how to build their theological debates around a single word, and, here in this passage, Paul masterfully does just that.

Paul goes on to explain how the agreement GOD made with Abraham could not be canceled 430 years later when HE gave the Law to Moses, because if GOD did that, HE would be breaking HIS OWN Covenant Promise (Vs.17-18). The Law was given to us to show us how far we had strayed from the glorious standards that GOD instilled within us when HE shared HIS nature with us, creating us in HIS OWN spiritual image, way back in the beginning (Gen. 1:27). However, this divine system of law was to last only until the first advent of CHRIST JESUS, the SEED to whom the promise was made (Gal. 3:19).

There is no conflict between GOD's Law and HIS promise. If the Law could have brought us new life, we could have been saved simply by just obeying it. However, since we are all prisoners of sin, the only way that we can receive GOD's promise, is by believing in what CHRIST has done for us (Vs. 21-22). And so, actually, the Law was used by GOD to keep us in a sort of "protective custody" until the day when JESUS completed HIS unique earthly assignment, by way of HIS vicarious sacrifice on the cross (v. 23). And when that mission was completed, all who have sinned, and thereby, been cursed by the Law of GOD (Deuteronomy 27:26), can be removed from that curse, simply by believing in CHRIST JESUS.

All throughout Paul's ministry he returned again and again to the same point; The solutions to the enigmas of human life has always been in having and maintaining an experiential relationship of friendship with GOD, and, in continued faith in GOD. GOD's covenant with Abraham was made possible because of Abraham's faith in GOD, as the Law, at that time, did not yet exist.

The Law served only as our guardian and teacher, guiding us until CHRIST came, and now that HE has come, our salvation lies in our faith in HIM. We no longer need the Law as our guardian, now the HOLY SPIRIT guides those who believe in Christ JESUS (Vs. 24-25).

We are children of GOD, only through our faith in CHRIST. When we become one with CHRIST in baptism we are made like HIM, and are expected to emulate HIM through our behavior at all times. And weather we are Jew or Gentile, rich or poor, male or female, becomes irrelevant. Also, when we belong to CHRIST, we become the true children of Abraham, and the heirs to all of the promises that GOD gave to him (Vs. 26-29).

CHAPTER FOUR:

(16)

GOD'S CHILDREN THROUGH FAITH

Galatians 4:1-7

4 **(1) Now I say,** *That* **the heir, as long as he is a child, differeth nothing from a servant, though he be lord of all;**
(2) But is under tutors and governors until the time appointed of the father.
(3) Even so we, when we were children, were in bondage under the elements of the world:
(4) But when the fullness of the time was come, GOD sent forth HIS SON, made of a woman, made under the law,
(5) To redeem them that were under the law, that we might receive the adoption of sons.
(6) And because ye are sons, GOD hath sent forth the SPIRIT of his SON into your hearts, crying, Abba, FATHER.
(7) Wherefore thou art no more a servant, but a son; and if a son, then an heir of GOD through CHRIST.

COMMENTARY:

In Galatians chapter 4, verses 1-7, Paul continues to expound on his point that we are children of GOD only through our faith in CHRIST. In first century Israel, the process of growing up was far more definite than it has ever been in American life.

Back then, on the twelfth birthday of a Jewish male, his father would take him into the synagogue, and on that day, the boy would become a "Son of the Law", after certain religious oaths and rituals. He would then, quite literally, become responsible for his own actions before GOD. There was then established, a clear boundary line between the boy that was, and the man that now is. Literally overnight, the boy became a man.

When the male was under the age of twelve, he was a mere child in the eyes of the Jewish Law, and therefore, under the rule, or dominion, of the

Laws of his parents. But when he became of age, he was freed from under their rule, and became fully responsible for making his own decisions, and, could also claim his inheritance from them. That's how it was with us before CHRIST came.

We were under the spiritual rule of this world, literally slaves to sin. But when GOD sent CHRIST to be born of woman into a world of sin, and subject HIMSELF to the Law (as a 100% human being), HE also represented for us, the one and only chance we had to be freed from under the dominion of sin, death, and the Law.

As a 100% human being, JESUS perfectly obeyed the laws of GOD, simply because HE shared GOD's "nature", (just as all human beings do), even before the HOLY SPIRIT ever descended upon HIM at the River Jordan, following HIS baptism by John. At that point, HE had already lived a perfect life for 30 years, and HE obeyed HIS FATHER GOD completely, because it was HIS desire to do so. In other words, JESUS proved, quite literally, that we, as human beings, don't obey GOD because we don't desire to do so, and not, because we can't help it!

HE made it possible for all mankind to be adopted into the family of GOD as HIS OWN children, and thus, believers become heirs to everything that CHRIST HIMSELF has.

PAUL'S CONCERN FOR THE GALATIANS
Galatians 4:8-20

4 **(8) Howbeit then, when ye knew not GOD, ye did service unto them which by nature are no gods.**
(9) But now, after that ye have known GOD, or rather are known of GOD, how turn ye again to the weak and beggarly elements, whereunto ye desire again to be in bondage?
(10) Ye observe days, and months, and times, and years.
(11) I am afraid of you, lest I have bestowed upon you labour in vain.
(12) Brethren, I beseech you, be as I *am*; for I *am* as ye *are*: ye have not injured me at all.
(13) Ye know how through infirmity of the flesh I preached the gospel unto you at the first.

(14) And my temptation which was in my flesh ye despised not, nor rejected; but received me as an angel of GOD, *even* as CHRIST JESUS.
(15) Where is then the blessedness ye spake of? for I bear you record, that, if *it had been* possible, ye would have plucked out your own eyes, and have given them to me.
(16) Am I therefore become your enemy, because I tell you the truth?
(17) They zealously affect you, *but* not well; yea, they would exclude you, that ye might affect them.
(18) But *it is* good to be zealously affected always in *a* good *thing*, and not only when I am present with you.
(19) My little children, of whom I travail in birth again until CHRIST be formed in you,
(20) I desire to be present with you now, and to change my voice; for I stand in doubt of you.

COMMENTARY:

In verses 8-20, we see Paul's deep concern for the Galatians, who, not long ago, were literally slaves to "pagan gods" that did not exist in the natural sense. And now that "they had found salvation in the real GOD" (knew GOD on a personal level), or rather, "the real GOD had gracefully given HIS salvation to them", they seemed to be "falling back" into the clutches of those same weak, spiritual forces that they had just left behind. They were also, at one and the same time, trying to win favor with the "true GOD" by adhering to the "Jewish calendar" of ritual celebrations and observances such as "Passover", "Pentecost", and the "tabernacles festivals" (the Law).

Salvation from man's perspective is that "he has found GOD" (confession with the mouth), however, salvation from GOD's perspective is that "HE has found us" (when we accept HIM in the heart). In verse 8 Paul tells the Gentile believers that they were slaves to false gods before they discovered the "Real GOD", or rather, "the Real GOD found them". He then asks (v.9), "Why do you want to go back again and become slaves once more to the weak and useless spiritual powers of this world?".

Like many "professed" Christians in today's society, the Galatians were trying to endear themselves to GOD by going to church, or worship services for a couple of hours every Sunday, or every Sabbath day, while all through the remainder of the week, they ignored GOD completely, by way of their worldly behavior, and lifestyles. However, true Christians know that true worship of GOD can only be exemplified in our day to day and actions, attitude, and behavior.

Paul had become concerned that all of his "hard work" and teaching meant nothing to them. In verse 11 Paul uses the Greek term "kekopiaka" which means "to labor to the point of exhaustion, in vain". He wanted to know, "Where was the zeal for CHRIST, and the love and care that they had shown him" when he first brought them the Good News on his first missionary journey with Barnabas?

At that time, even though Paul was sick with a revolting ailment, they did not reject him, but rather, they treated him as though he were an angel, or even, CHRIST HIMSELF. And now, they were treating him as if he were an enemy, because he was teaching them the truth (Vs.13-15).

To live in CHRIST is to be "free" from the gravitational pull of this world, and that does not just mean free from the lure of the things of the world (idol gods, people, etc.), but also, it means to be free from the bondage of sin and death (permanent separation from GOD), and, free from the law (V.12).

The false teachers who had followed Paul and Barnabas into Galatia had apparently won many of the Galatians over. And now, upon writing this letter, Paul felt as though he was going through "labor pains" all over again, needing to de-program them, to get them back to the "right teaching" that they had originally accepted from him. He, No doubt, felt that they needed to be released, once again, from the spiritual chains of sin and death that had formerly bound them to the world. And, he felt that he had to try and extricate them with his only weapon coming in the form of the words of this powerful letter.

THE TWO CHILDREN OF ABRAHAM
Galatians 4:21-31

4 **(21)** Tell me, ye that desire to be under the law, do ye not hear the law?
(22) For it is written, that Abraham had two sons, the one by a bondmaid, the other by a freewoman.
(23) But he *who was* of the bondwoman was born after the flesh; but he of the freewoman *was* by promise.
(24) Which things are an allegory: for these are the two covenants; the one from the mount Sinai, which gendereth to bondage, which is Agar.
(25) For this Agar is mount Sinai in Arabia, and answereth to Jerusalem which now is, and is in bondage with her children.
(26) But Jerusalem which is above is free, which is the mother of us all.
(27) For it is written, Rejoice, *thou* barren that bearest not; break forth and cry, thou that travailest not: for the desolate hath many more children than she which hath an husband.
(28) Now we, brethren, as Isaac was, are the children of promise.
(29) But as then he that was born after the flesh persecuted him *that was born* after the SPIRIT, even so *it is* now.
(30) Nevertheless what saith the scripture? Cast out the bondwoman and her son: for the son of the bondwoman shall not be heir with the son of the freewoman.
(31) So then, brethren, we are not children of the bondwoman, but of the free.

COMMENTARY:

In the first century, many Jews believed that Paul's teachings on grace and salvation by faith, seriously undermined the "Mosaic Law", and thus, denied GOD's Old Testament revelation to man. Paul argued instead, that, the Gospel he taught only served to uphold the Law, and to give it the place that GOD always intended for it to have.
In Galatians chapter 4, taking up at verse 21, Paul sets out to educate the early Christian Church in Galatia and other places on how GOD's grace and salvation through JESUS CHRIST actually establishes the Law in

GOD's intended role, which is, to be a mirror that can, first, show us our sins, and then, point us toward faith.

In the Greek, the word New Testament writers use for "faith" is "pistis", and it means "to rely upon with an inward certainty". Even before the Law, there was Faith. Abraham is the towering figure to whom the Jews traced their origins and special place as "GOD's chosen people".

Here in this passage, Paul once again demonstrates from sacred history, that, salvation always has been a gift of GOD received through faith, and that, faith is the way by which Abraham received his salvation, even before there was a Law, or a "Ten Commandments". Righteousness was accredited to Abraham, because he had faith, and he believed GOD.

In the biblical Greek, there is a wonderful sounding word that New Testament writers use for "promise". It is "epaggelia" (ep-ang-el-ee-ah), and it is "an announcement of divine assurance of good". Now Paul points out to the Gentiles of the church at Galatia that Abraham had two sons, one (Ishmael) from his "servant wife, Hagar, and the other (Isaac) from his "freeborn wife, Sarah. He tells them that the son of Hagar was born as a result of a "human attempt" to bring about fulfillment of "GOD's promise". However, the son of Sarah was born as a result of GOD's OWN fulfillment of HIS OWN promise (Vs.21-23).

Paul argues that, the "promise" of GOD was given to Abraham because of his "faith". And since the promises that are given to him, and, to his offspring are rooted in faith, and not, in the law, the Gentiles too then, must also rely on faith, rather than works, or the law, in order to please GOD, and continue to receive HIS "promised goodness".

Sarah and Hagar serve as an illustration of GOD's two covenants. Hagar represents Mount Sinai where people first became enslaved to the Law. Today Jerusalem is like Mount Sinai in Arabia because she and her children live in slavery. But Sarah, the free woman, represents the new heavenly Jerusalem. It is she who is our mother, and therefore, we are also children of the "promise", just like Isaac (Vs. 24-28).

Abraham was confident that GOD was able to do that which HE had promised, and, that HE would surely keep HIS word. Whenever we believe GOD's promise of salvation through JESUS CHRIST, we too, are accredited with "righteousness" that we did not, or could not earn on our own (Romans 4:18-25).

If salvation depended on us we would surely be lost, however, since our salvation depends on GOD keeping HIS promise to those who believe, we have the greatest of all possible guarantees.

Paul used Abraham as an example, because the Jews regarded him as the father of their race, and the earthly pattern of what a man should live like. Paul was seeking to prove that, what makes a man righteous, is not his works, or obedience to the Law, but rather, it is his faith and trust in GOD.

Paul also used Abraham as an example, because, he himself, was a wise teacher who could discern human thoughts. He recognized that faith is abstract, and, that the human mind finds it very difficult to grasp abstract ideas.

Using Abraham as an example was Paul's way of personifying faith, and thereby, developing a better understanding of what is needed, if we are to please GOD. And his use of Sarah and Hagar was to show how we must "get rid of the flesh", as Abraham had to do with his wife, Hagar, and "cling to the SPIRIT, as he kept Sarah, the wife and mother of the "promised son", Isaac.

We are not children of the servant girl who was obligated to the Law, but rather, we are children of the freewoman, acceptable to GOD, because of our faith. We must, in our human minds, receive and accept by faith, the divine and abstract ideas of GOD, WHO HIMSELF is Spirit, and therefore abstract, and HE dwells in Heaven. To trust and believe GOD is necessary, not just for the people in Paul's day, nor, just for the Jews, but rather, for all people, for all time.

CHAPTER FIVE:

(23)

FREEDOM IN CHRIST
Galatians 5:1-15

5 **(1) Stand fast therefore in the liberty wherewith CHRIST hath made us free, and be not entangled again with the yoke of bondage.**
(2) Behold, I Paul say unto you, that if ye be circumcised, CHRIST shall profit you nothing.
(3) For I testify again to every man that is circumcised, that he is a debtor to do the whole law.
(4) CHRIST is become of no effect unto you, whosoever of you are justified by the law; ye are fallen from grace.
(5) For we through the SPIRIT wait for the hope of righteousness by faith.
(6) For in JESUS CHRIST neither circumcision availeth any thing, nor uncircumcision; but faith which worketh by love.
(7) Ye did run well; who did hinder you that ye should not obey the truth?
(8) This persuasion *cometh* not of HIM that calleth you.
(9) A little leaven leaveneth the whole lump.
(10) I have confidence in you through the LORD, that ye will be none otherwise minded: but he that troubleth you shall bear his judgment, whosoever he be.
(11) And I, brethren, if I yet preach circumcision, why do I yet suffer persecution? then is the offence of the cross ceased.
(12) I would they were even cut off which trouble you.
(13) For, brethren, ye have been called unto liberty; only *use* not liberty for an occasion to the flesh, but by love serve one another.
(14) For all the law is fulfilled in one word, *even* in this; Thou shalt love thy neighbour as thyself.
(15) But if ye bite and devour one another, take heed that ye be not consumed one of another.

COMMENTARY:

Whenever we turn to the LORD, the "veil" that prevents us from understanding the truth is removed. Our minds are no longer hardened, and so, now we begin to perfectly understand the things of GOD, that we had previously failed to comprehend. This veil can only be removed by the "SPIRIT", whenever we start to believe in the "Risen SAVIOR", JESUS CHRIST.

"And now the LORD is that SPIRIT, and wherever the SPIRIT of the LORD is, there is "freedom" (2 Corinthians 3:17). Everyone who has had the veil removed can now be "free" to be the mirror that brightly reflects the glory of the LORD. And as the SPIRIT of the LORD works within us, we become more and more like GOD, and reflect HIS glory even more, to others, in the world, through our behavior.

Here in Galatians chapter 5, verses 1-15, Paul reminds the Christians at the Church in Galatia of their newly found "freedom in CHRIST", and encourages them to remain free, and to not get tied up again in the "slavery of the LAW" (v.1). The Christian life is a life apart from law and license, and it is, instead, a life lived according to the SPIRIT. To turn to the law does five things, says Paul, and they are all negative to the Christian Believer;

- It ruins grace (Vs.1-2)
- It makes a person a debtor (v.3)
- It causes one to fall away from grace (Vs.4-6)
- It blocks the progress of those who believe (Vs.7-10)
- It nullifies the purpose of the Cross (Vs.11-12)

The Galatians, who had been influenced by the "false teachers" who had infiltrated the church since Paul had left the area, had begin to rely on "circumcision" and other Jewish rituals and observances to make them "right" with GOD, instead of their faith in CHRIST. They did not realize that, by doing these things, they were actually "cutting themselves off from CHRIST, and thereby, from GOD's grace (Vs.2-4).

In the Greek, the word "apokaradokia" is the term used for "earnest expectation", or "hope for the future". We, who live by the SPIRIT, eagerly anticipate "the first signs of the coming of the glory of GOD" (CHRIST's return). We look with "high expectations" to receive everything that GOD promises those who are right with HIM, through our faith in CHRIST. When we place our faith in CHRIST, it makes no difference to GOD whether we are circumcised or not. What is important is that we have an undying faith that expresses itself through "love" (Vs.5-6).

Paul warned that it takes only one person to infect all the others (v.9) in the church, and he said he was trusting in GOD to rescue them back to the right path. He knew too, that, GOD would judge those responsible for leading the church astray, by confusing the people and mixing the "holy with the profane" in the church, in word, thought, and, in deeds (v.10).

The Gentiles in the church at Galatia needed to realize that the Jews were persecuting Paul because he preached against the doctrine of Judaism, which supported the belief in the law and good works. He was never a component of circumcision for Gentiles, which GOD charged only to the Jews, and no one else.

The "freedom" that Christians are called to, is not the freedom to satisfy our "sin nature", but rather, it is the freedom to satisfy the "nature of GOD" that is within us, by serving one another in love. The whole law of GOD can be summed up into one command; "Love your neighbor as yourself". It is high time that we become aware of how we're destroying each other by choosing to live in the prison (world) that is, outside of CHRIST JESUS.

LIVING BY THE SPIRIT'S POWER
Galatians 5:16-26

5 **(16)** *This* I say then, Walk in the SPIRIT, and ye shall not fulfill the lust of the flesh.

(17) For the flesh lusteth against the SPIRIT, and the SPIRIT against the flesh: and these are contrary the one to the other: so that ye cannot do the things that ye would.

(18) But if ye be led of the SPIRIT, ye are not under the law.

(19) Now the works of the flesh are manifest, which are *these*; Adultery, fornication, uncleanness, lasciviousness,

(20) Idolatry, witchcraft, hatred, variance, emulations, wrath, strife, seditions, heresies,

(21) Envyings, murders, drunkenness, revellings, and such like: of the which I tell you before, as I have also told *you* in time past, that they which do such things shall not inherit the kingdom of GOG.
(22) But the fruit of the SPIRIT is love, joy, peace, longsuffering, gentleness, goodness, faith,
(23) Meekness, temperance: against such there is no law.
(24) And they that are CHRIST's have crucified the flesh with the affections and lusts.
(25) If we live in the SPIRIT, let us also walk in the SPIRIT.
(26) Let us not be desirous of vain glory, provoking one another, envying one another.

COMMENTARY:

In the biblical Greek, the word used for "world" is "kosmos", and it is from that word that we derive our English word "cosmos". In the spiritual sense, it is that complex intertwining of sinful desires that shape our world of "lost humanity".

When we choose the "Christian Walk" we should automatically become strangers to worldly behavior. We are no longer permanent residents of this earth, but rather, we become citizens of Heaven, and therefore, the laws of GOD should become paramount to us. It is not until we fall in love with goodness that "wrong things" will no longer fascinate, and have power over us. Our relationship with GOD then becomes our greatest asset. By contrast, the person who loses his or her heart to the things of this world is the person most vulnerable to satan.

The end of all things earthly is near, for each of us, personally. For, that is the warning in the messages that the ancient prophets, and, the New Testament writers and thinkers, all leave us with. And those warnings are just as valid today as they ever were. In this day and age, both the HOLY SPIRIT of GOD, and the Bride (the true Christian Church) are beckoning us to come out of the world (Rev. 22:17), however, unfortunately, the lure of this world, and satan, are beckoning us to stay and indulge ourselves with our "sin nature".

The HOLY SPIRIT in us will always seek to compel us towards CHRIST. However, the "sin nature" within us, will always try and tug us back toward the world. That battle that wages on inside of each of us, between "the reason to do right", and "the passion to want to do wrong", will continue to stay with us, long after we accept the gift of salvation. However, through our strength in CHRIST, we can ultimately overcome the "gravitational pull of this world", just as CHRIST did, and find our place in "the ultimate happy ending" that has been prepared for us by GOD, since the foundation of this world.

In Galatians 5, verses 16-21, the Apostle Paul advises Christians to choose to live their new lives in the HOLY SPIRIT, as opposed to returning to their old life of doing what their sinful nature dictates to the flesh. Here Paul gives us a "catalog of evil things" that we are to have "self-control" ("egkrateia"/eng-krat-i-ah) against, while yet living in this world. While certainly we have to exist in the world physically, we don't have to participate in its Luciferic agenda.

Contrary to the beliefs of most Christians, our call is not to try and "make the world a better place", but rather, it is a call by GOD to, first, remove ourselves from the world spiritually, and then, help to extract others, leading them out of the darkness of this world and into the light of CHRIST. The world belongs to satan at this point, and this world, since the beginning has never improved from one generation to the next, not even during JESUS' first advent.

The earth is where GOD planted HIS "vineyard", and HE entrusted mankind by giving him dominion over it. Man ceded it over to satan in the Garden of Eden, and caused sin and death to enter into the world. Since then, all throughout scripture, the "vineyard" is never mentioned apart from the idea of "degeneration", it has never gotten better, though many a man has tried. Down through the ages man has failed to recognize what his one assignment from JESUS is, and that is "to draw men from the world" that he has already given over to satan, and "make them disciples of JESUS", and JESUS HIMSELF will make the world a better place, when HE returns. That's HIS job, not ours.

Back in verse 1 of this chapter of Galatians, Paul reminded us that our "Christian Freedom" does not mean that we have freedom in indulge in the trappings of the lower side of human life, but rather, it is freedom to walk in the true life that can only be found in CHRIST JESUS, and in our reliance on the power of the HOLY SPIRIT of GOD to guide us. Here in this passage (Vs. 16-21), every word that Paul uses in his list of evil doings has a very vivid picture associated with it.

- **"Adultery" and "fornication"**, for instance, is quite literally the opposite of chastity, which true Christianity requires from all of us as people made in the spiritual image of GOD.
- **"Uncleanness"**; Here Paul uses the Greek word "akatharsia" which describes the pus of an unclean wound.
- **"Lasciviousness"**; from the Greek word "aselgeia", which means, readiness for any immoral, lustful pleasures, or, to be sinfully out of control.
- **"Idolatry"**, which is the worship of anything, or anyone, other than GOD".
- **"Witchcraft"**; it literally means the use of drugs, which in ancient times was a necessary part of sorcery.
- **"Enmity"**, the complete opposite of love, it describes one who is characteristically hostile to someone else.

All together Paul mentions no less than seventeen fruits of evilness that the "human sin nature" can easily cotton to. Anyone, who chooses to indulge in any of these "works of the flesh", unless they repent, can never enter into the Kingdom of Heaven.

Starting in verse 22, the Apostle Paul shares with us a list of "lovely things" that characterize the "fruit of the SPIRIT". The catalog includes;

- Love,
- Joy,
- Peace,
- Patience,
- Kindness,
- Goodness,
- Fidelity,
- Gentleness,
- Self-control.

The HOLY SPIRIT is the engine that drives the converted person's "new self" in the opposite direction of their "old self", away from their "sin nature". HE also produces in the converted person's personality, the "fruits of the SPIRIT" that are mentioned here by Paul.

These GODly qualities replace the unGODly desires for the "fruits of evil" that had previously "dominated the thought process and actions" of the now "converted person". It then becomes the responsibility of that converted person to keep in step with the HOLY SPIRIT (Gal. 5:25). He or she must then "live by the SPIRIT", and "be led by the SPIRIT" responding only to HIS promptings, as HE seeks to guide our decision-making in every area of our lives. We must, in our hearts, show our reliance on the SPIRIT, and our confidence in "doing what we know to be right". Our lives will then no longer be marked by our sinful acts, but rather, it will be marked by the deeds of one who is submissive to the SPIRIT of GOD.

CHAPTER SIX:

WE REAP WHAT WE SOW
Galatians 6:1-10

6 (1) Brethren, if a man be overtaken in a fault, ye which are spiritual, restore such an one in the spirit of meekness; considering thyself, lest thou also be tempted.
(2) Bear ye one another's burdens, and so fulfill the law of CHRIST.
(3) For if a man think himself to be something, when he is nothing, he deceiveth himself.
(4) But let every man prove his own work, and then shall he have rejoicing in himself alone, and not in another.
(5) For every man shall bear his own burden.
(6) Let him that is taught in the word communicate unto him that teacheth in all good things.
(7) Be not deceived; GOD is not mocked: for whatsoever a man soweth, that shall he also reap.
(8) For he that soweth to his flesh shall of the flesh reap corruption; but he that soweth to the SPIRIT shall of the SPIRIT reap life everlasting.
(9) And let us not be weary in well doing: for in due season we shall reap, if we faint not.
(10) As we have therefore opportunity, let us do good unto all *men*, especially unto them who are of the household of faith.

COMMENTARY:

In the Greek, the word used for "restore" is "katarizo" (kat-a-rid-zo), and it is a "medical term" that is used to describe anything from "re-setting a broken bone", to "mending a fishing net". As the believer becomes spiritually mature, we are expected to then go out and help restore someone else who has gone astray (Gal. 6:1), or lead someone else out of the "darkness of this world", by introducing them to the "light of CHRIST".

We are to help those who are broken, to heal and mend. Our job is not to try to expose them to shame, or, to overlook the damage that sin has done in their lives, and the lives of those who are close to them.

Paul wanted Christians to exhibit the "fruit of the SPIRIT" in their everyday lives, and not get caught up in the kind of "self-righteousness" that could come from the practice of "legalism". The "humility" that it takes to help people grow in the Christian Faith, and then guard against going astray, could not be found in the practice of legalistic "Judaism". The responsible Christian must seek to help those who are caught up continually in sin. They do not seek to criticize or "pile it on" those who have gone away from GOD, or, who have never known GOD. They, instead, seek to help "restore" them back to the path of righteousness, because they realize that, as humans, we are all capable of falling to various temptations in life.

"We are our brother's keeper", and we must all help carry each other's burdens. All Christians have burdens, and they can include such things as health challenges, financial needs, family, etc., and some are simply caught under the weight of "wrongdoings". However, in any situation, we need to help those Christians who have stumbled beneath the weight of the pressures of this world.

JESUS tells us that we will be judged according to our reaction to human need (Matt. 25:31-46), and the greatest human needs are the needs for a person "to be forgiven", "to obey GOD", and "to maintain an experiential, personal relationship with GOD", at all times.

We simply cannot ignore the ways and plan of GOD, and get away with it. For, GOD has dealt a tragic existence to those who choose to live without HIM. The burden that those who are "lost" in this world have to carry is the awareness that "something more" exists in this life. To aid them in their struggle, or frustrating inability to figure out just what that "something" is, is the task that CHRIST JESUS has charged us with. We all need, or have needed each other's help in that regard, at one time, or the other, in our life. That is because we are created with a capacity for eternal things, in other words, we share GOD's nature.

We all must come to a crossroad where we come face to face with the realization that this life cannot be all that there is. Sin, is what has cut us off from eternity, and darkened our understanding, and will to obey GOD.

And JESUS, through HIS vicarious sacrifice on the cross, offers us a chance to re-connect with the Almighty GOD.

Most of us will come to know what a burden it is to yearn for eternity, and yet, not know GOD. And so we, at one time or another will need help from someone else, or will have an opportunity to help someone along in their Christian Walk.

The way that we respond to those in need, constitutes the kind of "seeds" that we are sowing. If, we sow "good seeds", in this life, our "good crops" will be reaped abundantly at the appropriate time, in the Kingdom of Heaven. However, if we do not sow good seeds, in this life, our "bad crops" will be burned in the pits of Hell, in the life to come.

PAUL'S FINAL ADVICE TO THE GALATIANS
Galatians 6:11-18

6 **(11)** Ye see how large a letter I have written unto you with mine own hand.

(12) As many as desire to make a fair shew in the flesh, they constrain you to be circumcised; only lest they should suffer persecution for the cross of CHRIST.

(13) For neither they themselves who are circumcised keep the law; but desire to have you circumcised, that they may glory in your flesh.

(14) But GOD forbid that I should glory, save in the cross of our LORD JESUS CHRIST, by WHOM the world is crucified unto me, and I unto the world.

(15) For in CHRIST JESUS neither circumcision availeth any thing, nor uncircumcision, but a new creature.

(16) And as many as walk according to this rule, peace *be* on them, and mercy, and upon the Israel of GOD.

(17) From henceforth let no man trouble me: for I bear in my body the marks of the LORD JESUS.

(18) Brethren, the grace of our Lord JESUS CHRIST *be* with your spirit. Amen.

COMMENTARY:

In Paul's final advice to the Galatians he points out to them that he is closing out his letter in his own handwriting, not that of his personal scribe. He again stresses some of the issues that he had previously discussed in this letter. These final words contain both a summary, and, advice on how to proceed in the future, as far as their dealings with detractors go.

Detractors and false teachers, for the most part, go along with the program of man, either because they fear persecution from man for teaching the truth of GOD's word (they are cowards), or, because they are more interested in "glorifying themselves" by influencing people to "follow them", instead of following CHRIST (Vs. 11-13).

"True men of GOD" refuse to boast about anything except what JESUS CHRIST did on the cross, in order that HE might save us from eternal damnation. Paul says that "it is because of the cross that his interest in the things of this world died long ago, and the world's interest in him died along with it (v.14).

When we choose the Christian Walk, it is the "circumcision of the heart" that becomes paramount, not the "physical circumcision" of the male's sexual organ. If that was the key, then women would be blocked from salvation. What counts is whether we really have been changed into a new creature because our "heart", ("kardia" in the Greek, which means "our thinking" has been changed), to the thoughts of "the things that are important to GOD", and away from those "things that are important to the world" (v.15).

Paul's body bore the scars that served as evidence that he belonged to CHRIST JESUS. And if we are to follow JESUS' example as Paul did, we too, can only follow that example, by "going through the cross" (suffering for the cause of CHRIST JESUS). GOD expects us to suffer for the faith we say we hold, until we can began to believe in our thinking (heart), that we really do hold it, because GOD, WHO knows all things, knows through HIS infinite wisdom that, if our faith costs us nothing, then, we are in danger of valuing it at "nothing".

HOME AND CHURCH BIBLE STUDY

COMMENTARIES FROM

PAUL'S

LETTER TO

THE

EPHESIANS

LARRY D. ALEXANDER

INTRODUCTION TO THE BOOK OF EPHESIANS

In the first century Ephesus was the "queen city" of Asia. Unfortunately, it was also Asia's center of the popular cult of "Artemis" (Diana). Artemis was the most popular of the many idol gods that found their home in the city of Ephesus. In fact, the worship temple of Artemis was one of the great wonders of the world in the first century, and thousands of visitors traveled to Ephesus each year to get a glimpse of this imposing, and structurally beautiful edifice.

The priesthood of Artemis used their great wealth to become bankers, receiving deposits, and also making sizable loans to individuals, groups, and governments. Artemis worshipers represented the most "materially successful" religion in the world at that time, but they were also the most "spiritually deplete" individuals in the world at that time.

Ephesus was also a center for "witchcraft", "sorcery", and "the occult", and it all served as the backdrop for what Paul would be up against when he dared to bring the doctrine of Christianity to this "demonic hotbed" of religion and superstition.

Paul wrote this letter during his first imprisonment in Rome, circa A.D. 60-61. It was one of three doctrinal "jailhouse letters" (the others were Colossians and Philippians) that were believed to be written by Paul while he was awaiting trial there. He had earlier spent three years in Ephesus (probably A.D. 54-57) and had had a great impact on that city, and other communities throughout the Roman province of Asia. Thousands of people had converted to Christianity during Paul's stay there, and thousands of dollars worth of books and paraphernalia on magic, were publicly burned and destroyed.

Here in this letter, Paul presents an overview of the history of creation where, even before time began, GOD had already worked out HIS plans for the world. He then moves to that present-day first century when GOD first begin saving people through CHRIST JESUS, and later, into a future time, when all evil will be overcome, this also, by JESUS CHRIST.

The book of Ephesians is perhaps, the highest reach of "the Christian thought", and maybe that's because it harps so strongly on the "love" theme. In fact, in this profound doctrinal letter, we see the Greek "noun form" of "love", "agape" being used 9 times, and its "verb form", "agapao" being used 10 times. It literally begins and ends with the idea, or thought, of "unconditional love". But perhaps more than anything else, it also teaches that Jewish and Gentile believers are "united in CHRIST, and that they must demonstrate their love for one another, and, for the GOD WHO created and then "saved" us, from ourselves.

CHAPTER ONE:

SPIRITUAL BLESSINGS

1 ⁽¹⁾ **Paul, an apostle of JESUS CHRIST by the will of GOD, to the saints which are at Ephesus, and to the faithful in CHRIST JESUS:**
⁽²⁾ **Grace** *be* **to you, and peace, from GOD our FATHER, and** *from* **the LORD JESUS CHRIST.**
⁽³⁾ **Blessed** *be* **the GOD and FATHER of our LORD JESUS CHRIST, who hath blessed us with all spiritual blessings in heavenly** *places* **in CHRIST:**
⁽⁴⁾ **According as HE hath chosen us in HIM before the foundation of the world, that we should be holy and without blame before HIM in love:**
⁽⁵⁾ **Having predestinated us unto the adoption of children by JESUS CHRIST to HIMSELF, according to the good pleasure of HIS will,**
⁽⁶⁾ **To the praise of the glory of HIS grace, wherein HE hath made us accepted in the beloved.**
⁽⁷⁾ **In whom we have redemption through HIS blood, the forgiveness of sins, according to the riches of HIS grace;**
⁽⁸⁾ **Wherein HE hath abounded toward us in all wisdom and prudence;**
⁽⁹⁾ **Having made known unto us the mystery of HIS will, according to HIS good pleasure which HE hath purposed in HIMSELF:**
⁽¹⁰⁾ **That in the dispensation of the fullness of times HE might gather together in one all things in CHRIST, both which are in heaven, and which are on earth;** *even* **in HIM:**
⁽¹¹⁾ **In whom also we have obtained an inheritance, being predestinated according to the purpose of HIM who worketh all things after the counsel of HIS OWN will:**
⁽¹²⁾ **That we should be to the praise of HIS glory, who first trusted in CHRIST.**
⁽¹³⁾ **In whom ye also** *trusted,* **after that ye heard the word of truth, the gospel of your salvation: in WHOM also after that ye believed, ye were sealed with that HOLY SPIRIT of promise,**
⁽¹⁴⁾ **Which is the earnest of our inheritance until the redemption of the purchased possession, unto the praise of HIS glory.**

COMMENTARY:

The Christian Church is not one that is born of bricks and mortar, but rather, it is born of the living flesh of JESUS CHRIST. Instead of being stocked with silver and gold, it is stocked with spiritual blessings from on High. And instead of being overseen by an earthly priest; it is overseen and headed, by the LORD HIMSELF. Therefore, it does not lie at the mercy of hostile spiritual forces, but rather, it is ultimately guarded and protected by a supreme and powerful GOD.

The opening verses of Paul's letter to the Ephesians gives us visions of a child who is surrounded by gifts at Christmas time. One can easily feel how GOD wishes to give us all the needed blessings that are promised to those who belong to HIS adopted family. When we belong to the family of GOD, JESUS opens up the doors to HIS FATHER's wealth and security, and helps us to fully understand HIS "house rules", or, HIS will, and HIS ways.

In Ephesians 1, verses 3-14, after a warm and wonderful greeting, the Apostle Paul lays out "three provisions of spiritual blessings" by the GODHEAD (GOD the FATHER, GOD the SON, and GOD the HOLY SPIRIT). In the original Greek writing, this particular passage (verses 3-14), is one long sentence. It contains a trio of blessings that are bestowed upon anyone whose heart belongs to CHRIST JESUS. They are;

- <u>The selection of the FATHER (Vs. 3-6)</u> – GOD has blessed us with every spiritual blessing in the heavenly realms, simply because we belong to CHRIST. Before HE made the world, GOD loved and chose us in CHRIST to be holy (set apart) and without fault in HIS eyes. HIS immutable plan has always been to adopt Gentiles into HIS family, through JESUS CHRIST, and HE finds great pleasure in doing so.
- <u>The sacrifice of the SON (Vs. 7-12)</u> – GOD, through HIS rich kindness, purchased our freedom through the blood of HIS only begotten SON, and as a result, our sins are forgiven. In addition HE has given us wisdom and understanding, as "HIS secret plan", the "Christian Church", consisting of both Jews and Gentiles united together in CHRIST, has been revealed to the world. Because of

CHRIST JESUS, WHO is the "HEAD of the Church" and everything else in Heaven and on Earth, we receive an inheritance from GOD. GOD's purpose is that, we who trust in CHRIST should praise HIM, for HE is our glorious SAVIOR.

- <u>The seal of the HOLY SPIRIT (V.13-14)</u> – When we first heard the truth of the Gospel of CHRIST, and believed, HE identified us as HIS OWN by giving us the HOLY SPIRIT, GOD's promise, guarantee, and "seal".

Before GOD ever created the world, HE already had in place, special plans for those HE would later call to partake in HIS great and wonderful work. The rewards we receive at the end of our "Christian walk" are greatly increased in accordance to how close we walked in obedience to the MASTER. HIS "secret plan" (the church) has now been revealed to us, and it centers on CHRIST JESUS, HIS only begotten SON. And "at the right time", HE will bring everything together under the authority of HIS SON, indeed, everything in Heaven, and, on earth.

It is because of CHRIST JESUS, that we have received an inheritance from GOD, and GOD chose us, from the beginning. All things happen now, just as GOD planned them long ago, and when we believe in CHRIST, GOD identifies us as HIS OWN. And HE gives us HIS HOLY SPIRIT to guide us and hold us by the hand, so that when we stumble, we will not fall. The HOLY SPIRIT is "GOD's guarantee" that HE will grant us everything that HE has promised, and, that HE has purchased us at a high price to be in HIS family. This is just one more reason for us to praise GOD at all times, not just with our lips, but indeed, most importantly, through our daily behavior, which is the true sign of worship.

PAUL'S PRAYER FOR SPIRITUAL WISDOM
Ephesians 1:15-23

1 (15) Wherefore I also, after I heard of your faith in the Lord Jesus, and love unto all the saints,
(16) Cease not to give thanks for you, making mention of you in my prayers;

(17) That the God of our Lord Jesus Christ, the Father of glory, may give unto you the spirit of wisdom and revelation in the knowledge of him:
(18) The eyes of your understanding being enlightened; that ye may know what is the hope of his calling, and what the riches of the glory of his inheritance in the saints,
(19) And what *is* the exceeding greatness of his power to us-ward who believe, according to the working of his mighty power,
(20) Which he wrought in Christ, when he raised him from the dead, and set *him* at his own right hand in the heavenly *places*,
(21) Far above all principality, and power, and might, and dominion, and every name that is named, not only in this world, but also in that which is to come:
(22) And hath put all *things* under his feet, and gave him *to be* the head over all *things* to the church,
(23) Which is his body, the fullness of him that filleth all in all.

COMMENTARY:

Paul had continually prayed for the church at Ephesus every since he heard of their strong faith JESUS CHRIST and their love for Christians everywhere. He prayed for their "spiritual wisdom", and, that they would use the "spiritual resources" that we all have, as believers in CHRIST, to grow in the knowledge of GOD.

Paul's "intercessory prayers" in Ephesians, as well as Colossians help us to know, and gives us guidance, as to how we can pray for others who serve in the body of CHRIST. He prayed that their hearts and thoughts would be "flooded with the light" of CHRIST, so that they would truly grasp the promise of the wonderful future that GOD calls us to, as Christians. GOD wants us to really recognize the "rich" and "glorious" inheritance that HE gives to those who believe in CHRIST JESUS, our LORD.

JESUS CHRIST was "raised up" into sovereign power, and Paul wanted Christians to understand that the incredible greatness of that power is more than just "resurrection power". It is the power that catapulted

JESUS into a place of supremacy at the right hand of GOD the FATHER (Vs.19-20).

Now JESUS is far greater than any ruler or authority or anything else in this world, or, the world to come. All things have been put under the authority of JESUS CHRIST for the benefit of the Church, HIS body. The "True Church", which exists only in those who believe, is filled by the omnipresence of JESUS, our LORD and SAVIOR, and shares, or has access, to that power, whenever, and wherever, we need it (Vs.21-23).

CHAPTER TWO:

WE ARE MADE ALIVE WITH CHRIST
Ephesians 2:1-10

2 **(1) And you *hath HE quickened*, who were dead in trespasses and sins;**
(2) Wherein in time past ye walked according to the course of this world, according to the prince of the power of the air, the spirit that now worketh in the children of disobedience:
(3) Among whom also we all had our conversation in times past in the lusts of our flesh, fulfilling the desires of the flesh and of the mind; and were by nature the children of wrath, even as others.
(4) But GOD, WHO is rich in mercy, for HIS great love wherewith HE loved us,
(5) Even when we were dead in sins, hath quickened us together with CHRIST, (by grace ye are saved;)
(6) And hath raised *us* up together, and made *us* sit together in heavenly *places* in CHRIST JESUS:
(7) That in the ages to come HE might shew the exceeding riches of HIS grace in *HIS* kindness toward us through CHRIST JESUS.
(8) For by grace are ye saved through faith; and that not of yourselves: *it is* the gift of GOD:
(9) Not of works, lest any man should boast.
(10) For we are HIS workmanship, created in CHRIST JESUS unto good works, which GOD hath before ordained that we should walk in them.

COMMENTARY:

In the Greek, the word used for "world" is "kosmos". It is from this word that we derive our English word "cosmos". In the spiritual sense, it describes that complex intertwining of sinful desires that shape our world of lost humanity.

When we choose the Christian walk, we automatically become strangers to worldly behavior. We are no longer permanent residents of this earth, but rather, we become citizens of Heaven, and therefore, the laws of GOD should become paramount to us, in other words, GOD begins to dominate our thought process. We then "change our mind", or "repent" from our former "worldly way" of thinking. We, in a very real sense, begin to "share the mind of CHRIST".

In the biblical sense, the word "heart" is translated from the Greek word "kardia" which describes one's "thoughts" or "way of thinking", not one's emotions. Still, our conversion is often treated as "an emotional experience of psychological change". And even though here in Ephesians 2, Paul correctly depicts "conversion" as a "spiritual transformation", or, "a metamorphosis" from a state of "spiritual death" to "spiritual life", this passage does have some psychological implications.

Before our conversion to Christianity, we generally follow the ways of the world and are driven by sinful thoughts and desires. And while, even after conversion, we still are capable of sin, our lives are, for the most part, re-oriented toward GOD, through the power of the HOLY SPIRIT. However, all in all, it is not until a person actually falls in love with goodness, that wrong things, no longer fascinate, and have power over them.

The reality of our inward change, must, in time, be reflected in a true change of lifestyle, or the supposed conversion is not real. And so, our relationship with GOD remains the Christian's greatest asset, and the person who loses their heart to the things of this world, is the person most vulnerable to satan.

The end of all things is near, for each of us, personally. For, that is the warning in the messages that the ancient prophets, and New Testament writers and thinkers, all leave us with. And those warnings are as valid today as they ever were. Human nature has long been corrupted and we tend to desire to create a god in our own image, instead of worshipping the GOD, WHO made us in HIS divine image.

The GOD of our salvation through JESUS CHRIST is the only GOD, and theologians often debate whether it is salvation or faith that HE grants to us freely. But the true Christian has faith that the gift of salvation is an example of how GOD's grace is greater than all of our sins combined. Paul tells us that GOD acted graciously to grant salvation to each of us, who believe, and no amount of good deeds can earn us what GOD freely gives.

GOD determined long ago to form the Christian Church out of the flawed humanity that is "us". He always took those of us who were "dead in sin" and made us "alive in CHRIST JESUS". HE, quite literally, re-fashions us to make us suitable for every good work that HE has prepared for us to do, and through JESUS, HE closed the gap between us and HIMSELF, and brought us back into "a personal relationship of friendship with HIM".

GOD sees the unbeliever who is walking with satan, and thereby, in step with this current generation, or, world-way of thinking. HE desires to exchange their "life of misery", and, at best, "temporal happiness", for "a life that is filled grace, mercy and spiritual riches".

Salvation, and GOD's continued abundant grace, is available to all people, but one has to voluntarily choose to become a partaker, in GOD's grace. Every human being has the opportunity to be made alive with CHRIST, to be in oneness and peace with CHRIST, and, be a temple for the LORD, our GOD in Heaven.

JEWS AND GENTILES ARE ONE IN JESUS CHRIST
Ephesians 2:11-22

2 (11) Wherefore remember, that ye *being* in time past Gentiles in the flesh, who are called Uncircumcision by that which is called the Circumcision in the flesh made by hands;
(12) That at that time ye were without CHRIST, being aliens from the commonwealth of Israel, and strangers from the covenants of promise, having no hope, and without GOD in the world:
(13) But now in CHRIST JESUS ye who sometimes were far off are made nigh by the blood of CHRIST.
(14) For HE is our peace, WHO hath made both one, and hath broken down the middle wall of partition *between us*;
(15) Having abolished in HIS flesh the enmity, *even* the law of commandments *contained* in ordinances; for to make in HIMSELF of twain one new man, *so* making peace;
(16) And that HE might reconcile both unto GOD in one body by the cross, having slain the enmity thereby:
(17) And came and preached peace to you which were afar off, and to them that were nigh.
(18) For through HIM we both have access by one SPIRIT unto the FATHER.

(19) Now therefore ye are no more strangers and foreigners, but fellow citizens with the saints, and of the household of GOD;
(20) And are built upon the foundation of the apostles and prophets, JESUS CHRIST HIMSELF being the chief corner *stone*;
(21) In WHOM all the building fitly framed together groweth unto a holy temple in the LORD:
(22) In WHOM ye also are builded together for a habitation of GOD through the SPIRIT.

COMMENTARY:

In Ephesians 2, taking up at verse 12, the Apostle Paul talks about "the state of the Gentile before CHRIST". Here Paul states "five disadvantages" of the pre-CHRIST Gentile and he doesn't include "circumcision" in his list. Paul never considered circumcision to be a necessary act (Acts 15) for Gentiles to partake in, in order to become a follower of CHRIST JESUS. At least one of the items on this list is also shared by the Jewish believers. On Paul's list of reminders to the Gentiles we find that before CHRIST;

- Gentiles, like Jews were living apart from HIM.
- Gentiles were excluded from GOD's people, Israel.
- Gentiles did not share in the promises of GOD.
- Gentiles lived without knowledge of GOD's Will.
- Gentiles were without hope.

GOD, through HIS wisdom, determined that HE would form HIS "new Church" out of "flawed material" (mankind), because HE loved us, even as we were, still sinners, deeply embedded in our own transgressions. HE began this process by recreating us, in and through, HIS SON, JESUS, and as a result, HE effectively closed the spiritual gap between the Jews and the Gentiles.

Before JESUS' vicarious sacrifice on the cross redeemed all mankind in general, and all Christians, in particular, the Jews had enjoyed "a special covenant relationship with GOD" that the Gentiles were not privy to. JESUS came to usher in a "New Covenant" from GOD. It is a covenant that is far superior to any, before, or since that time. It is the duty of the Christian (Jews and Gentiles) to build his or her foundation on that "Most High Faith" (Christianity), learning to pray in the power of the HOLY SPIRIT, and never again forgetting the conditions of that covenant, under which the love of GOD has called us. And then, finally, we must all, still, wait on mercy from JESUS CHRIST unto eternal life.

By bringing Jews and Gentiles together through the cross, JESUS effectively settled the longstanding feud between the only two races that ever mattered. Now, both Jews and Gentiles are fellow citizens and members of GOD's divine household and holy temple (the Christian Church). JESUS HIMSELF has made us all one people under GOD (V.14).

In verses 15-18 we see that CHRIST, the PEACEMAKER and Jew, died for the Gentile, and by doing so, "HE removed the barrier that is Jewish Law", a barrier to both races of people that was mistakenly viewed as the way to GOD, by the Jews. HE opened up the way for both to be joined together as "one new man" in the body of CHRIST. Christianity serves as "peace" to anyone who wishes to become a living part of it. In it we can find peace with GOD, and, peace among each other.

The thought of being "built together for GOD's dwelling" (v.22) is a wonderful one, and even though every believer is "saved" individually, each person also immediately becomes a part of "a greater body in CHRIST JESUS", WHO is the Church. Together, Christians (Jews and Gentiles) are the people whom GOD indwells with HIS HOLY SPIRIT. Through us, HE is able to display HIS glory, and thereby, we possess the divine opportunity to show the whole world that Christianity really does produce the best men and women.

In the Christian Church, JESUS makes a place for all mankind to enter into the family of GOD. And the Church can only realize its unity when it understands fully that it cannot exist apart from CHRIST JESUS. It has to provide a home for the SPIRIT of CHRIST to dwell in, and an opportunity for every man, woman, and child to meet, in that SPIRIT.

CHAPTER THREE:

GOD'S SECRET PLAN REVEALED
Ephesians 3:1-13

3 **(1)** For this cause I Paul, the prisoner of JESUS CHRIST for you Gentiles,
(2) If ye have heard of the dispensation of the grace of GOD which is given me to you-ward:
(3) How that by revelation HE made known unto me the mystery; (as I wrote afore in few words,
(4) Whereby, when ye read, ye may understand my knowledge in the mystery of CHRIST)
(5) Which in other ages was not made known unto the sons of men, as it is now revealed unto HIS holy apostles and prophets by the SPIRIT;
(6) That the Gentiles should be fellow heirs, and of the same body, and partakers of HIS promise in CHRIST by the gospel:
(7) Whereof I was made a minister, according to the gift of the grace of GOD given unto me by the effectual working of HIS power.
(8) Unto me, who am less than the least of all saints, is this grace given, that I should preach among the Gentiles the unsearchable riches of CHRIST;
(9) And to make all *men* see what *is* the fellowship of the mystery, which from the beginning of the world hath been hid in GOD, who created all things by JESUS CHRIST:
(10) To the intent that now unto the principalities and powers in heavenly *places* might be known by the church the manifold wisdom of GOD,
(11) According to the eternal purpose which he purposed in CHRIST JESUS our LORD:
(12) In WHOM we have boldness and access with confidence by the faith of HIM.
(13) Wherefore I desire that ye faint not at my tribulations for you, which is your glory.

COMMENTARY:

When Paul wrote this letter to the Ephesians, he was under house arrest by the order of the Emperor Nero in Rome. And whereas he was allowed to have visits from his friends and collegues, he was still chained to the wrist of a prison guard at all times.

It is with this scenario in mind that we approach the opening line of this passage where Paul says, "I am a prisoner of CHRIST JESUS because of my preaching to the Gentiles" (v.1) (NLT). What Paul is really saying is that "he is a prisoner for the cause of CHRIST JESUS".

JESUS had given Paul a special mission of announcing HIS "favor of salvation" to the Gentiles, and had revealed to him "the secret plan" of GOD. The secret plan that provided us with JESUS CHRIST as the SAVIOR for the whole world, not just the Jews, had now been set into motion.

The New Covenant, the Christian Church, would include both Jews and Gentiles into its body, which would spiritually and physically resemble the body of CHRIST, literally. It was a plan that had never been revealed to the Old Testament prophets, and the saints of previous generations. However, now, GOD was revealing it by the power and presence of the HOLY SPIRIT, to all who choose to "receive it" and come to CHRIST in these latter days (Vs.2-5).

Paul's charge from CHRIST was to announce that the Gentiles have an "equal share" with the Jews in all of the spiritual riches inherited by "GOD's chosen people". Both groups can now, by believing the Good News, become a part of the same body, and enjoy together, the promise of blessing, through CHRIST JESUS our LORD (v.6).

In this passage, Paul re-visits the thought which serves as the "motif", or "theme" for this letter. In his original Greek writing, the phase "energeian dynameos" used in verse 7 means "mighty power". Here Paul is sharing with us, how he is responding to the special favor and power of GOD by counting it a "privilege" to serve CHRIST JESUS with his whole life, to the death, spreading the Good News. He had been given the privilege of being the first man to know of GOD's secret plan, and he had been given the privilege to be the first to make that plan known to the newly found Christian Church. And most of all, Paul clearly understood that he had done nothing to deserve it, in fact, he considered himself to be the least deserving of all Christians (v.8).

Paul says that he was chosen to explain to everyone, the secret plan that GOD, the CREATOR of all things, had from the beginning. In other words, GOD did not come up with this plan as a last result, when everything else concerning man had gone wrong. GOD, WHO knows all things, knew from the beginning what HE wanted to do in this particular space in time. GOD's purpose was "to show HIS wisdom, in all of its rich variety" (sophia polypoikilos), to all of the rulers and authority on earth, and in the Heaven realms (Vs.9-10).

GOD's wisdom is manifested through the Christian Church by the joining together of Jews and Gentiles in one body under CHRIST JESUS. This represents GOD's "eternal plan" being carried out through JESUS CHRIST our LORD. Because of JESUS, and our faith in HIM, we can now reconnect into a right relationship of family and friendship with GOD the Father. We now have "direct access" to HIM, through JESUS CHRIST, our LORD, and we need not despair anymore.

PAUL'S PRAYER FOR SPIRITUAL EMPOWERING
Ephesians 3:14-21

3 **(14) For this cause I bow my knees unto the FATHER of our LORD, JESUS CHRIST**
(15) Of WHOM the whole family in heaven and earth is named,
(16) That HE would grant you, according to the riches of HIS glory, to be strengthened with might by HIS SPIRIT in the inner man;
(17) That CHRIST may dwell in your hearts by faith; that ye, being rooted and grounded in love,
(18) May be able to comprehend with all saints what *is* the breadth, and length, and depth, and height;
(19) And to know the love of CHRIST, which passeth knowledge, that ye might be filled with all the fullness of GOD.
(20) Now unto HIM that is able to do exceeding abundantly above all that we ask or think, according to the power that worketh in us,

(21) Unto HIM *be* glory in the church by CHRIST JESUS throughout all ages, world without end. Amen.

COMMENTARY:

JESUS came to show man the difference between "parenthood" and "fatherhood". Parenthood or "Paternity" means "father", purely in the "physical sense". It is a term that can be used even of a man who has never really seen or spent time with his child at all. However, "fatherhood" is a term that is much more dynamic, because it describes a man who is intimately involved with his offspring. To merit this description, a man has to have an experiential relationship of love and caring with his child.

Before JESUS came, man could only see GOD in a "paternal sense". However, when JESUS came, HE presented us with a "physical picture" of ONE WHO knew GOD the FATHER on a personal, experiential level. It is on this level that Paul had also come to know GOD, and he wanted everyone in the Christian Church to understand the kind of new relationship and power that they now found themselves having access to through the HOLY SPIRIT.

In Ephesians 3, verses 14-21 Paul prays for "a mighty spiritual empowerment from GOD" on the Church at Ephesus. Here we see a petition for five spiritual qualities, or "powers" that would energize the members of the body of CHRIST in any age;

- "That <u>GOD's people may gain a mighty inner strength</u>" from the HOLY SPIRIT – Here, in the Greek for "mighty", "krataiothenai" (krat-ah-yo-then-ahee) - "the power to overcome resistance", and "inner strength", "dynamis", which is "dynamic living power and strengthened love" (v.16).
- "That <u>CHRIST would be more at home in our hearts</u>" – "katoi-kesai" (kat-ohee-kes-ahee) which means "to dwell ongoing", or, "to remain with" (v.17).

- "That GOD's people be given the power to understand" – "exischusete" (ex-is-khoo-se-te), which means, "to be entirely competent and able", or "to possess inherent strength" (v.18).
- "That GOD's people may experience the love of CHRIST" – Know CHRIST experientially (v.19a).
- "That GOD's people may be filled with the fullness of life and power that comes from GOD" (V.19b).

GOD is the true template of "fatherhood" that all men should seek to follow, but, in order for us to do that, we must first ask "THE PATTERN MAKER" to empower and embody us with a "SPIRITUAL POWER" from on high, that would allow us to become the kind of leaders that HE calls us to be.

Like a good FATHER, GOD has given us an identity, and HE has also given us, HIS only begotten SON, JESUS CHRIST, to dwell in our hearts, the moment we first believe. And, as if that weren't enough, HE, in addition, strengthens and empowers us with HIS HOLY SPIRIT, because HE desires very badly, that we become successful in overcoming this world, just as JESUS did, so that we might find ourselves in the ultimate happy ending, that has been prepared for us by HIM, since the foundation of this world.

CHAPTER FOUR:

(51)

UNITY IN THE BODY
Ephesians 4:1-16

4 ⁽¹⁾ I therefore, the prisoner of the LORD, beseech you that ye walk worthy of the vocation wherewith ye are called,
⁽²⁾ With all lowliness and meekness, with longsuffering, forbearing one another in love;
⁽³⁾ Endeavouring to keep the unity of the SPIRIT in the bond of peace.
⁽⁴⁾ *There is* one body, and one SPIRIT, even as ye are called in one hope of your calling;
⁽⁵⁾ One LORD, one faith, one baptism,
⁽⁶⁾ One GOD and FATHER of all, WHO *is* above all, and through all, and in you all.
⁽⁷⁾ But unto every one of us is given grace according to the measure of the gift of CHRIST.
⁽⁸⁾ Wherefore HE saith, When HE ascended up on high, HE led captivity captive, and gave gifts unto men.
⁽⁹⁾ (Now that HE ascended, what is it but that HE also descended first into the lower parts of the earth?
⁽¹⁰⁾ HE that descended is the same also that ascended up far above all heavens, that HE might fill all things.)
⁽¹¹⁾ And HE gave some, apostles; and some, prophets; and some, evangelists; and some, pastors and teachers;
⁽¹²⁾ For the perfecting of the saints, for the work of the ministry, for the edifying of the body of CHRIST:
⁽¹³⁾ Till we all come in the unity of the faith, and of the knowledge of the SON of GOD, unto a perfect man, unto the measure of the stature of the fullness of CHRIST:
⁽¹⁴⁾ That we *henceforth* be no more children, tossed to and fro, and carried about with every wind of doctrine, by the sleight of men, *and* cunning craftiness, whereby they lie in wait to deceive;
⁽¹⁵⁾ But speaking the truth in love, may grow up into HIM in all things, which is the head, *even* CHRIST:

(16) From whom the whole body fitly joined together and compacted by that which every joint supplieth, according to the effectual working in the measure of every part, maketh increase of the body unto the edifying of itself in love.

COMMENTARY:

In Ephesians chapter 4, verses 1-16, the Apostle Paul urges us to maintain attitudes that express love and unity within the Body of CHRIST, which is the Church. In the Greek the word Paul uses for "worthy" in verse 1 is "axious" and it literally means "to balance the scale". Here Paul is saying that we must give "equal weight" to our calling and conduct. We must make an effort to practice what we preach, and our doctrine must be balanced with our lifestyle.

This passage, along with Romans 12:1 and 1 Corinthians 12 constitutes "the Christian image of the holy Body of CHRIST". Whenever a person joins themselves to a society or faith, they must obligate themselves to change or adapt to a living style that is compatible in that society, or faith. People who choose to join the body of CHRIST must adapt their style of living into a way that is compatible with GOD's Word. We must work on being "humble" and "gentle, and also be "patient" and "loving" to those who are our "neighbors", who are also living in the "community of GOD" (v.2).

In verses 4-6 we find no less than seven theological elements of the Christian Church. There we see that;

- We are all one body
- We have the same SPIRIT
- We have all been called to the same glorious future
- There one LORD
- There is one Faith
- There is one Baptism
- There is one GOD and FATHER over us all, in us all, and living through us all

JESUS, the ONE WHO descended from Heaven to this lowly earth in order to usher in to us, "a brand New Covenant" from GOD, is also the ONE WHO gives us all certain gifts that should be used to enhance, improve, nourish, and grow HIS Body, the Church. The apostles, prophets, evangelists, pastors, and teachers are responsible for equipping GOD's people to do HIS work and build the Church to the point where we are unified in Faith and knowledge of JESUS CHRIST, and, are mature and full grown in the LORD. Our goal is to measure up to the example that CHRIST JESUS showed us as a 100% man, during HIS life here on earth (Vs.11-13).

GOD does not wish for us to continue to act like children who can't make up their minds about what they believe. HE doesn't wish for us to fall prey to the cleaver liars who make their deceitful words sound like the truth (v.14). And if we are able to hold fast to the truth, becoming more and more like CHRIST, the whole Body will be fitted together perfectly as each part (person) does their own specially assigned work. By performing our own special work assignment to the best of our GOD-given ability, we will also be helping the other parts of the Church to grow so that the whole Body is healthy and operational, and filled with love (v.15-16).

To waver back and forth like a ship lost at sea, is not the life of a true Christian. Each member of the Body of CHRIST must grow and mature and reflect GOD's image to others through our own behavior, by standing firm in GOD's Word. Satan will always plant people in the Church who will try to introduce his agenda through the things that are popular in the world, such as miming (witch craft), worldly music, trunk or treat, trunk fest, fall festivals and other things that parallel Halloween, etc., but serious, mature Christians must resist such influences in the Church, and, in their personal lives.

The Church must function like a body because it is a body, the Body of CHRIST. It needs all of its parts to be working properly, held together by "love" if it is to have a productive spiritual life, and grow by GOD's standard of success, not the world's standard. And we should always remember that, most importantly, the one thing that will keep the Church healthy and efficient, is by it maintaining an intimate and personal connection to JESUS CHRIST, WHO is the head, brains, mind, and SPIRIT of the Body. The Church has never needed our human ingenuity to operate successfully. It only needs us to share the gifts with the Church that GOD has so graciously given us, and it is incumbent upon us to know the difference. We don't need to try and improve upon that which GOD has already perfectly set up. We just need to be obedient and do things the way GOD says do it. And when we take the time to study the plan of GOD, we'll find that it is not open to our own personal interpretation, but rather, we'll find that "the Word of GOD interprets itself to us".

LIVING AS CHILDREN IN THE LIGHT
Ephesians 4:17-32

4 **(17)** This I say therefore, and testify in the LORD, that ye henceforth walk not as other Gentiles walk, in the vanity of their mind,
(18) Having the understanding darkened, being alienated from the life of GOD through the ignorance that is in them, because of the blindness of their heart:
(19) Who being past feeling have given themselves over unto lasciviousness, to work all uncleanness with greediness.
(20) But ye have not so learned CHRIST;
(21) If so be that ye have heard HIM, and have been taught by HIM, as the truth is in JESUS:
(22) That ye put off concerning the former conversation the old man, which is corrupt according to the deceitful lusts;
(23) And be renewed in the spirit of your mind;
(24) And that ye put on the new man, which after GOD is created in righteousness and true holiness.
(25) Wherefore putting away lying, speak every man truth with his neighbour: for we are members one of another.
(26) Be ye angry, and sin not: let not the sun go down upon your wrath:
(27) Neither give place to the devil.
(28) Let him that stole steal no more: but rather let him labour, working with *his* hands the thing which is good, that he may have to give to him that needeth.

(29) Let no corrupt communication proceed out of your mouth, but that which is good to the use of edifying, that it may minister grace unto the hearers.
(30) And grieve not the HOLY SPIRIT of GOD, whereby ye are sealed unto the day of redemption.
(31) Let all bitterness, and wrath, and anger, and clamour, and evil speaking, be put away from you, with all malice:
(32) And be ye kind one to another, tenderhearted, forgiving one another, even as GOD for CHRIST's sake hath forgiven you.

COMMENTARY:

The Christian Church is the body of CHRIST and GOD's only representative in the world. The members of that body are people who were once ungodly in their behavior, and were hopelessly confused and void of any useful aim or goal. We were people whose minds were full of darkness, and we were far away from living the life that GOD calls for us to live through HIS Word. We didn't care about right or wrong, and we had given ourselves over to immoral ways and desires. We were people whose lives were filled with greed and all kinds of impurities.

In Ephesians 4, verses 17-24, the Apostle Paul makes an appeal to the new believers at the Church at Ephesus to start "living as children of the light". Here in this passage Paul spells out some of the characteristics of living as pagans, or unbelievers, with lifestyles that are contrary to GOD.

Believers are taught the ways of CHRIST so that they may be able to leave their old unacceptable lifestyles behind. Children of GOD have to be able to cast off their old "sinful evil nature" in order to re-capture "the nature of GOD" with which they were born, and most lose, before they ever realize that they have it.

There has to be a "spiritual renewal of thoughts and attitude", or a "transformation of the heart" before we can display the "nature of GOD" which we received when HE made us in HIS OWN likeness, in the beginning. We must be righteous, holy, and true to our "GODly nature", that we get to uncover, because of what JESUS has done for us, through HIS vicarious sacrifice.

In verses 25-32 Paul gives us a list of things that we must absolutely rid ourselves of if we are to live as children of the LIGHT;

- "We must put away all "falsehood"", that means both "spoken and unspoken lies" (silently standing by letting someone believe something that is untrue), dishonesty and deceit (v.25).
- "Do not sin by letting anger take control over you" (v.26a).
- "Do not let the sun go down while you are still angry", because anger gives a foothold to the devil" (v.26b-27).
- "If you are a thief, stop stealing", Instead, start using your hands to give generously to those in need (v.28).
- "Do not use foul or abusive language". Let everything you say be good and helpful, so that your words will be an encouragement to those who hear them (v.29).
- "Do not grieve the HOLY SPIRIT by the way you live". HE is the ONE WHO identifies you as HIS OWN, guaranteeing that you will be saved on the "Day of Redemption" (v.30).

Verse 31 represents a "summation" or "recap", as well as a "blanket statement" covering those things that were not mentioned in verses 25-30. Here we see that we have to absolutely "clean the house" of our former wicked ways if we are to live as children who are walking in the light for all to see. Paul says we are to get rid of;

- **All bitterness**
- **All rage (thymos)**
- **All anger (orge)**
- **All harsh words (krauge)**
- **All slander (blasphemia)**
- **All malicious behavior (kakia)**

All these things must be banished from the Christian life. We must shed these ungodly practices as if they were an old garment no longer fit to wear, and no longer useful for where we now reside.
We must, instead, be kind to each other (v.32), by being "tenderhearted" (eusplanchnoi), "forgiving" (charizomenoi) one another, just as GOD

forgives us, because it grieves the HOLY SPIRIT, offends JESUS, and hurts GOD whenever we are hostile towards each other, instead of being kind to one another.

CHAPTER FIVE:

LIVING IN THE LIGHT
Ephesians 5:1-20

5 (1) Be ye therefore followers of GOD, as dear children;
(2) And walk in love, as CHRIST also hath loved us, and hath given HIMSELF for us an offering and a sacrifice to GOD for a sweet smelling savour.
(3) But fornication, and all uncleanness, or covetousness, let it not be once named among you, as becometh saints;
(4) Neither filthiness, nor foolish talking, nor jesting, which are not convenient: but rather giving of thanks.
(5) For this ye know, that no whoremonger, nor unclean person, nor covetous man, who is an idolater, hath any inheritance in the kingdom of CHRIST and of GOD.
(6) Let no man deceive you with vain words: for because of these things cometh the wrath of GOD upon the children of disobedience.
(7) Be not ye therefore partakers with them.
(8) For ye were sometimes darkness, but now *are ye* light in the LORD: walk as children of light:
(9) (For the fruit of the SPIRIT *is* in all goodness and righteousness and truth;)
(10) Proving what is acceptable unto the LORD.
(11) And have no fellowship with the unfruitful works of darkness, but rather reprove *them*.
(12) For it is a shame even to speak of those things which are done of them in secret.
(13) But all things that are reproved are made manifest by the light: for whatsoever doth make manifest is light.
(14) Wherefore HE saith, Awake thou that sleepest, and arise from the dead, and CHRIST shall give thee light.
(15) See then that ye walk circumspectly, not as fools, but as wise,
(16) Redeeming the time, because the days are evil.
(17) Wherefore be ye not unwise, but understanding what the will of the LORD *is*.

(18) And be not drunk with wine, wherein is excess; but be filled with the SPIRIT;
(19) Speaking to yourselves in psalms and hymns and spiritual songs, singing and making melody in your heart to the LORD;
(20) Giving thanks always for all things unto GOD and the FATHER in the name of our LORD JESUS CHRIST;

COMMENTARY:

In the biblical Greek, the term used for "word" is "logos" (log-os), and it, more or less, emphasizes the message of that which is spoken. In John chapter 1, the apostle expresses to us that our LORD and SAVIOR, JESUS CHRIST personifies the Word of GOD, in the flesh. Here he is trying to get us to understand that one of the key reasons for JESUS' first advent, was, and is, for "communication".
JESUS is the "Spoken Word", and the "Living Expression" of all that which GOD ever sought to communicate to us about HIMSELF. Here John is saying, particularly in verse 1, that, JESUS is both, "identical" to the GOD of the Old Testament concept, and yet, HE is also distinct from HIM. One can imagine how stunning this must have been to the people of the first century. Even today, many people have a problem with embracing this concept, which has now become familiar, and yet still remains just as mysterious as it ever was. Here though, we can see that, while the concept may be difficult, John's teaching seems to be very clear. He is saying here that JESUS existed eternally with GOD the FATHER, as one GOD, yet, with a distinct and separate personality. Those of us who understand the concept that unity in a family and marriage represents, can certainly grasp the concept of "unity as one" between the FATHER and the SON.
It is true that in human society, if someone hands someone else a gift, and that person doesn't perceive that gift to be real, then they probably aren't going to reach out and accept it. Our believing in GOD, in all of HIS fullness, can be likened to that. GOD is giving us the gift of eternal life through HIS only begotten SON, JESUS the CHRIST. Believing in HIM involves seeing HIM as real, and, as coming from GOD, and then, reaching

out and accepting HIM. By accepting JESUS, one also accepts GOD the FATHER's wonderful gift of eternal life in Heaven, and, at one and the same time, becomes what they weren't before, and that is, quite simply, "a child of GOD".

JESUS came into the world to teach us how to live our lives under GOD, and, to teach us how to die and live again, with GOD. HE taught us how to give and forgive, and, HE taught us how to love, and how to give thanks. John points to JESUS as being the "LIGHT of the world", a true light for all people. In HIM we see exactly what GOD is like, and only HE can usher us into GOD's OWN glorious presence, without fear, without guilt, and, without shame.

In Ephesians chapter 5, verses 1-14 the Apostle Paul relates to Christians about "living in the light" that CHRIST JESUS, our SAVIOR, brought into a world of darkness. Paul begins this chapter by urging us Christians to follow GOD's example in everything that we do. We should live a life filled with love for one another, following the examples of CHRIST WHO loves us, and, WHO gave HIMSELF up as a ransom for us, to nullify our sins, through HIS death on the cross. It was a sacrifice that was like sweet perfume to GOD (Vs. 1-2).

With every ounce of "worldly success" comes an equal measure of "pride". To the contrary, with every ounce of "GODly success" comes an equal measure of "humility". Every professed Christian must strive to be an imitator of GOD, simply because they claim to be GOD's Children. The more we conform to the world, the more prideful we become, but the more we are able to transform from the world's ways, to the ways and examples of CHRIST, the more humble we become.

There should be a very distinct and clear difference between the lifestyle of a Christian, and that of one who desires to be like the world. Darkness and light cannot co-exist in the same space. When the people in the community of GOD compromise their ways with the ways of the world, the distinction between the two are soon lost, and professed Christians are no longer able to properly represent CHRIST to anyone with any accuracy.

In Ephesians 5, verses 3-13, we see perhaps Scriptures greatest and clearest defining of the contrasting moral differences between "light" and "darkness, or "right" and "wrong" by GOD's standards. The vices or sins mentioned in verses 3-4 (sexual immorality, impurity, or greed, even obscene talk and dirty jokes) portray self worship and a lack of concern for others.

Remember, a greedy person is nothing but an idolater, because they chase after and worship the things of this world. We should not be fooled by those who try to excuse such a sin as this. Those who desire to follow CHRIST should not have even a hint of these evil elements in his or her life. Anyone who practices such immoralities cannot expect to enter into the Kingdom of CHRIST (the Millennial Kingdom), and of GOD in Heaven (v.5).

People who are comfortable in their own sin, and, who are offended by those who try to rebuke, correct, or expose them, have themselves, a favorite "scripture-based saying" that they like to use. They love to tell people, "You can't judge". However, in the Christian bible there are three separate and distinct types of judgment. Two of them GOD expects all Christians to be able to do, and the third is one that only GOD HIMSELF can do. In fact, even if we wanted to do this third type of judgment, our mere mortality prevents us from being able to do it. There is a different Greek word that is used to describe each of them. They are;

- "Anakrino" (judgment) – A self examination, using "GOD's standards" to see if we ourselves are in line with HIS Word and Will at any given time.
- "Diakrino" (judgment) – "Using GOD's standards" to examine anything, or anyone to determine, or discern, that which is right, from that which is wrong in that person, thing, or situation.
- "Krino" (judgment) – A judgment of "condemnation"; it is a judgment that only our superior GOD can make. No human being can make this type of judgment, even if they wanted to, because we are all, ourselves, people under judgment from GOD at all times.

In Ephesians 5:10-14, the Apostle alludes to the two, of the three judgments that GOD expects us to make. Here we see a clear example of our duty to judge ourselves (Anakrino Judgment), and others (Diakrino Judgment), by first, finding out what is pleasing to GOD, by closely examining HIS Word and Will for our lives (Vs.10-11).

By closely studying GOD's Word and finding out what we ourselves are doing wrong (examining ourselves), we'll be able to help others who are going astray, to get themselves into line with GOD's Word and Will also. Serious Christians should take no part in the worthless, evil deeds and darkness that now permeate and dominate this world. The Word of GOD says that Christians should instead, rebuke and expose such evil (v.11). In fact, we should not even talk about the shameful things that ungodly people do even in secret, but rather, we should let our light shine on them, through our GODly behavior, so that it can become clear that their way is not the way to go. And so our lifestyle and behavior can expose things that are not right with GOD better than anything we can ever say. And wherever the Christian light of CHRIST shines through us, it will automatically expose evil deeds and actions in others.

In verses 15-20 Paul advises all Christians to live depending only on the HOLY SPIRIT's power to guide us. Christians must commit to seeking GOD's ways on a daily basis, and, to living wisely and not foolishly as unbelieving people live (v.15).

In the Greek, the word Paul uses in verse 16 in his original writings, "exagorazomenoi" (ex-a-gora-zo-men-ohee), means "to buy up the time" or "to make the most of every opportunity". As vibrant Christians, we are to take advantage of every opportunity we get to do good things according to GOD's standards, especially in these evil days that we live in. We must "walk circumspectly" not being drunk or high on wine, liquor, or illicit drugs, but rather, by being filled with the HOLY SPIRIT of GOD, WHO was sent to us by JESUS CHRIST (Vs.17-18).

When we allow the HOLY SPIRIT to control us, we will be able to sings psalms and hymns and spiritual songs among ourselves, just as fervently as we used to sing blues, pop, disco, rock and roll, and hip hop songs, when we were "lost" in the world. And we will always give thanks for everything to GOD the FATHER in heaven, in the mighty and precious name of JESUS CHRIST, our LORD and SAVIOR (vs.19-20).

FAMILY MATTERS
Ephesians 5:21 – 33

5 **(21)** Submitting yourselves one to another in the fear of GOD.

(22) Wives, submit yourselves unto your own husbands, as unto the LORD.

(23) For the husband is the head of the wife, even as CHRIST is the head of the church: and HE is the SAVIOUR of the body.

(24) Therefore as the church is subject unto CHRIST, so *let* the wives *be* to their own husbands in everything.

(25) Husbands, love your wives, even as CHRIST also loved the church, and gave HIMSELF for it;

(26) That HE might sanctify and cleanse it with the washing of water by the Word,

(27) That HE might present it to HIMSELF a glorious church, not having spot, or wrinkle, or any such thing; but that it should be holy and without blemish.

(28) So ought men to love their wives as their own bodies. He that loveth his wife loveth himself.

(29) For no man ever yet hated his own flesh; but nourisheth and cherisheth it, even as the LORD the church:

(30) For we are members of HIS body, of HIS flesh, and of HIS bones.

(31) For this cause shall a man leave his father and mother, and shall be joined unto his wife, and they two shall be one flesh.

(32) This is a great mystery: but I speak concerning CHRIST and the church.

(33) Nevertheless let every one of you in particular so love his wife even as himself; and the wife *see* that she reverence *her* husband.

COMMENTARY:

In Ephesians 5:21-6:4, the Apostle Paul teaches on how to be controlled by the HOLY SPIRIT at home as he turns his focus to the two most important family life relationships, "husband and wife", and "parents and children". Here he defines how we should all strive to live as children walking in the light of CHRIST at home, as well as in church. In fact, what we do Monday through Saturday in our homes, and on our jobs away from the church, is more of testament to how we love and worship GOD, than what we do in church on Sunday morning.

After Paul establishes the overriding principle of us all submitting to one another out of reverence for CHRIST JESUS (v.21), he moves on to the specifics of the spiritual responsibility of each family member toward each other, and, towards CHRIST. Wives are to submit to their husbands as they do to the LORD (v.22). Husbands are the head of the wife, as CHRIST is the head of the Christian Church, which is HIS body (v.23a). The husband should show love for his wife, and be willing to give his life for her, just as CHRIST was willing to give HIS life for the church that HE so loves (v.23b). Husbands ought to love their wives just as they love their own bodies. In fact, husbands actually show that they love themselves, when, they love their wives, who they are spiritually at one with, in the LORD (v.28).

GOD calls for us to have a united, GODly home front. The Christian family's interactions with one another should reflect CHRIST and HIS interactions with the Christian Church, or, "Body of CHRIST". GOD fully intends for us to enjoy a harmonious, SPIRIT-guided family relationship in submission to HIM first, and then, to each other, starting in our own homes (v.21).

In the New Testament Greek, the word used for "submit" is "hupotasso" (hoop-ot-as-so) and it means "to be under obedience to". It is a word that carries a complex concept which needs to be defined by the context in which it is used. Here in this passage, there is no question of power, or position as it is in, say, Romans 13. In this particular passage, Paul calls for all believers to develop an attitude of submission, and a willingness to be responsive by yielding to each other, out of love for each other.

It would be remiss of us to read hierarchy into these verses, but rather, we should see this passage as a call for us to begin to develop a sensitivity toward each other that will help to extricate us from "pride", and enable us to function at all times, in a more, loving and caring manner.

Each partner in a marriage has a special "privilege". A husband's privilege is to put his wife first, after GOD, just as CHRIST did when HE was crucified for us on the cross by Roman method. The wife's privilege is to set the tone of submission by being responsive and caring. And neither partner lords over the other, but rather, each partner ministers to the other in their own GOD-given, special ways, for that is the "responsibility" that comes with the privilege.

CHAPTER SIX:

FAMILY MATTERS (continued)

6 ⁽¹⁾ Children, obey your parents in the LORD: for this is right.
⁽²⁾ Honour thy father and mother; (which is the first commandment with promise;)
⁽³⁾ That it may be well with thee, and thou mayest live long on the earth.
⁽⁴⁾ And, ye fathers, provoke not your children to wrath: but bring them up in the nurture and admonition of the LORD.

COMMENTARY:

In Ephesians 6:1-4, Paul addresses the relationship between parents and children. In the Greek, the normal word used for "right" is "dexios" (dex-ee-os), and it means "being on the right side of". Here in this passage, however, Paul uses the Greek term "dikaios" (dik-ah-yos) for "right", which means "the proper course to follow". Children are to submit themselves under the leadership and care of their parents until they move out and start a family of their own, or become responsible adults capable of making their own decisions, for it is the proper course to follow. However, GOD commands a child should always "honor" their parents, no matter how old the child is. In fact, it is the first commandment of the Decalogue (Ten Commandments) that carries a promise from GOD, and that promise is one of a long life, filled with blessings.

Paul ends this passage with an admonishment to fathers to not anger their children with harsh worldly and "ungodly treatment", but rather, they are to bring them up with the "GODly discipline and instruction" that can be found in the Word of GOD. Here in verse 4a Paul uses the Greek term "parorgizo" (par-org-id-zo) in his original Greek writings, for "provoke", and it means "to exasperate" or "make things worse, by what one does or says". In the home, the father must present a picture of the LORD to his children, through both his speech and behavior, to, and before them. How a child views his or her father has a profound effect on how they view GOD later on in life. By provoking our children to anger through unGODly treatment, we will ultimately "make things worse" for them later on in life.

The command to "Honor your father and your mother" is the first commandment that parents can use to introduce their children to the ways of GOD. If children respect their parents, they will respond positively to their nurturing. Through GODly nurturing, it becomes easier for a child to see GOD in their parents, and come to know and show reverence to GOD after they become adults. When they come to know GOD, through a personal, experiential relationship with their parents, it becomes much easier for them to have and maintain that same kind of relationship with GOD later in life. And thus, they can enjoy a long life on earth, because we have passed on to them, a legacy of faith, were they will desire to continue walking in the light of CHRIST, and know the importance of passing that legacy on to their own children.

SERVANTS AND SUPERIORS
Ephesians 6:5-9

6 (5) Servants, be obedient to them that are *your* masters according to the flesh, with fear and trembling, in singleness of your heart, as unto CHRIST;
(6) Not with eye service, as men-pleasers; but as the servants of CHRIST, doing the will of GOD from the heart;
(7) With good will doing service, as to the LORD, and not to men:
(8) Knowing that whatsoever good thing any man doeth, the same shall he receive of the LORD, whether *he be* bond or free.
(9) And, ye masters, do the same things unto them, forbearing threatening: knowing that your MASTER also is in heaven; neither is there respect of persons with HIM.

COMMENTARY:

The word "slave" or "slaves" is translated from the original language only twice in scripture, once in the O. T. (Jeremiah 2:14), and once in the N. T. (Revelation 18:13). In all other occurrences the word "servant" is translated from the original Greek and Hebrew text, not "slave".
The definition of the word ⍰ "slave" is that, it is, "one who is bound in servitude to another "without payment for services". The word "servant", on the other hand, is defined as "one who is employed to perform services" for another, and is paid a specified agreed amount for those services.

With that said, in biblical times, it was quite common for a person to trade menial services for money, food, land, or any other necessary or unnecessary things. In today's society that is called a "job".

"The borrower is always the servant of the lender" (Proverbs 22:7). When we get ourselves into debt, particularly due to greed, or envy of what others have, or any other GODly or ungodly reason, we become servants to our lenders, and our jobs. Probably with the exception of a house to live in, we probably should not borrow money, and if we can afford to pay cash for the house, it would be wise to do so.

In the spiritual sense, anyone who is not a servant to GOD is a slave or servant to man, whether they realize it or not. And oftentimes, in the biblical days, even the "children of the debtor" could end up paying for services that were rendered to their parents, or can end up working off the debts of their parents. When we are in financial debt, the lender owns a piece of us, and we, in effect, become their "servant". And even when the lender dies, we may become the servant of their "heirs" by way of their inheritance.

In Ephesians 6, verses 5-9 Paul speaks on the very necessary topic of the "relationship between servants and superiors". Here in this passage the apostle advises Christians that we must be careful to be GODly, even in those relationships, and even if that relationship is a covenant between believing and unbelieving parties.

The servant must always obey and respect their superiors on their jobs. We must serve them as sincerely as we would CHRIST JESUS (v.5). We should work hard, even when our superior is not watching us, simply because we are also servants of CHRIST, and want, very badly, to do the will of GOD (v.6). We must work with enthusiasm as if we were working for the LORD, rather than for the people we are indebted to, and the LORD will reward us for the good and honest things that we do, regardless of the extent of our indebtedness to others (Vs.7-8).

The work superiors also have a responsibility under GOD to treat their servants rightly. They must not oppress or threaten the people who work for them, especially those superiors who are also believers. They must remember at all times that they too, have a "SUPERIOR" WHO dwells in Heaven, and HE HIMSELF does not have any "favorites" among HIS people (v.9).

CALLED TO STAND FIRM

6 ⁽¹⁰⁾ Finally, my brethren, be strong in the LORD, and in the power of HIS might.
⁽¹¹⁾ Put on the whole armour of GOD, that ye may be able to stand against the wiles of the devil.
⁽¹²⁾ For we wrestle not against flesh and blood, but against principalities, against powers, against the rulers of the darkness of this world, against spiritual wickedness in high *places*.
⁽¹³⁾ Wherefore take unto you the whole armour of GOD, that ye may be able to withstand in the evil day, and having done all, to stand.
⁽¹⁴⁾ Stand therefore, having your loins girt about with truth, and having on the breastplate of righteousness;
⁽¹⁵⁾ And your feet shod with the preparation of the gospel of peace;
⁽¹⁶⁾ Above all, taking the shield of faith, wherewith ye shall be able to quench all the fiery darts of the wicked.
⁽¹⁷⁾ And take the helmet of salvation, and the sword of the SPIRIT, which is the word of GOD:
⁽¹⁸⁾ Praying always with all prayer and supplication in the SPIRIT, and watching thereunto with all perseverance and supplication for all saints;
⁽¹⁹⁾ And for me, that utterance may be given unto me, that I may open my mouth boldly, to make known the mystery of the gospel,
⁽²⁰⁾ For which I am an ambassador in bonds: that therein I may speak boldly, as I ought to speak.
⁽²¹⁾ But that ye also may know my affairs, *and* how I do, Tychicus, a beloved brother and faithful minister in the LORD, shall make known to you all things:
⁽²²⁾ Whom I have sent unto you for the same purpose, that ye might know our affairs, and *that* he might comfort your hearts.
⁽²³⁾ Peace *be* to the brethren, and love with faith, from GOD the FATHER and the LORD JESUS CHRIST.
⁽²⁴⁾ Grace *be* with all them that love our LORD JESUS CHRIST in sincerity. Amen.

COMMENTARY:

In Ephesians 6:10-18, the Apostle Paul closes out his letter to the Ephesians with a remarkably creative summary of his overall message to them. Here he paints a vivid picture of the spiritual resources one would have to clothe himself with, if he is to do battle with the unseen world of evil that dictates to our "sin nature", and manifests its negative results in our physical lives.

As Christians, we are waging the fight of our lives on a daily basis, and our opponent is not one who is visible to our physical eyes. And while certainly we can feel his assault on our bodies, sadly, we continue to fight a losing battle because we fail to correctly identify just who our assailant really is.

In order to wage a successful battle we must first realize that the enemy is not other people, but rather, it is satan himself. And if we are going to fight against this enemy, and win, we must turn our battles over to GOD. The battle with satan is a battle for our souls, and in order to overcome him, we must put on "the full armor of GOD".

In order to beat us, satan uses such weapons as "pride", "lust", "other people", and "doubt". If we are to make a successful stand against him, we must incorporate "truth", "righteousness", "peace", "faith", "salvation", and "the Word of GOD". In short, we must don the full armor of GOD daily. We cannot use carnal weapons and expect to defeat the evil one in our own natural strength. But by clothing ourselves with the full armor of GOD, we become more than conquerors through our strength in CHRIST JESUS.

When we equip ourselves with all that GOD provides us, we are well able to win the spiritual battles that we will inevitably have to wage every single day of our lives here on earth. Paul's colorful description of the battle attire of GOD, is cleverly likened to the panoply of a Roman soldier, because he wants to ensure that the people understand exactly what they are up against, and how GOD has already provided the resources needed to overcome such a formidable foe.

Warren Wiersbe once wrote, *"Sooner or later every believer discovers that the Christian life is a battleground, not a playground, and that he faces an enemy who is much stronger than he is, apart from GOD"*.

As Christians, and, as human beings, we face, on a daily basis, three weapons, that are perpetually exploited by satan:

- First, there is "the world", which refers to the systematic opposition to GOD that surrounds us everywhere we go.
- Then there is "the flesh" which is controlled by our own "sin nature" which we inherited from Adam's disobedience to GOD, and, that is opposed to GOD and can naturally do nothing to please GOD in any way.
- And then finally, there is the "evil spirit", the devil himself, who gets into us and manipulates our thoughts, and thus dictates our actions and deeds, causing us to make all sorts of ungodly decisions in life.

We should be eternally thankful to JESUS for salvation through HIS overcoming of "the world", "the flesh", and "the evil spirit" of satan. We do not have to fight for victory, because the victory is already won. Now, we only have to fight from the victorious standpoint that CHRIST JESUS has given us. And the HOLY SPIRIT enables us, by faith, to appropriate HIS victory for ourselves, when we choose to fight and pray in GOD's army, and, in the name, of CHRIST JESUS, our LORD and DELIVERER.

In Paul's closing words to the Ephesians he lets them know that he is sending Tychicus, his beloved brother in CHRIST, to encourage them, and, to let them know how he was getting along while he is incarnated there in Rome.

In his final words we find a blessing being called down from GOD, by Paul, upon the people at the Church in Ephesus. Here Paul calls for the "peace" of GOD (man's highest good), the "love" of GOD", the complete resting of "faith" in CHRIST, and the all-important "grace" of GOD, which sustains us all, to abide with them, forever.

(71)

HOME AND CHURCH BIBLE STUDY

COMMENTARIES FROM

PAUL'S

LETTER TO

THE

PHILIPPIANS

LARRY D. ALEXANDER

INTRODUCTION TO THE BOOK OF PHILIPPIANS

The city of Philippi was named after Philip II (382-336 B.C.) of Macedonia, by his son, "Alexander the Great". Philip captured the city from the Thracians in 358 B.C. It is located about 10 miles northwest of the seaport of Neopolis near a sting of rich gold and silver mines, and was a staging point for the "Battle of Actium" 31 B.C. It was also near there, that, Mark Anthony and Octavius (Caesar Augustus) defeated Brutus and Cassius after they had murdered the Roman Emperor, Julius Caesar in 44 B.C. Shortly after that, Philippi became a colony of the original Roman Empire.

After the "Battle of Philippi" circa 42 B.C., Mark Anthony ordered some of his Roman soldiers to reside in Philippi, and twelve years later Octavian compelled the displacement also, of a large number of people from Italy. These Italian residents, however, were given special privileges called "Italic Rights", which meant that, in return for their displacement, their new land would be considered a part of "Italian soil", or they would still be "citizens of Rome", and thereby, exempt from taxes.

It was in A.D. 52 that Paul first visited the city of Philippi, during his second missionary journey with Silas. It later became the first European city in which a Christian church was established. Lydia and her family (Acts 16:11-15), and later, the Philippian jailer and his household (Acts 16:16-36), were all converted to Christianity by Paul and Silas, during the two men's visit, and incarceration, there in Philippi.

Ironically, Paul wrote this letter to the Philippians, while jailed under house arrest in Rome, some 10 years later. It was written in response to the financial generosity of the Philippian Church, during and after his visit there in Macedonia. Paul says that, they were the only church to respond in such a way, when he delivered to them, the good news about CHRIST JESUS.

Paul testifies that the Philippians had already ministered to his needs on three earlier occasions, twice while he was in Thessalonica (Philippians 4:15-16), and once in Corinth (2 Corinthians 11:9). And now, during this imprisonment in Rome, the church at Philippi sends their pastor, Epaphroditus, to minister to him there. Epaphroditus personally expressed to Paul, the affection that the church had for him, and he also delivered yet another financial blessing to Paul, in an effort to make his incarceration more comfortable.

This letter to the Philippians has a tone that is both, personal and practical in its instructions. All throughout, we can see a theme building that is joyful, and encouraging. Christians who were at odds with each other, were encouraged to make amends, and all believers were encouraged to aspire to obtain, and maintain, the high standards of GOD in their lives, and to encourage others to do the same.

At this point, Paul is unsure whether or not, he will die during his incarceration in Rome, however, he declares that, if death does come, he assures the believers that he will rejoice in the presence of GOD, and if he does not die, he will continue to serve GOD to the best of his ability.

As we read through the words of Paul's letter to the Philippians, we are made aware, through his experiences, of those things that can bring us joy through times of tribulation. The outstanding way in which the verses of chapter 2 exalts CHRIST as someone who chose to come to earth to suffer a death by Roman method, on a cross, and was raised by GOD to the highest and most exalted place of all, at the right hand of GOD the FATHER, certainly makes it one of the most encouraging passages in all of Scripture.

CHAPTER ONE:

PAUL'S GREETING, THANKSGIVING, AND PRAYER
Philippians 1:1-11

1 ⁽¹⁾ **Paul and Timotheus, the servants of JESUS CHRIST, to all the saints in CHRIST JESUS which are at Philippi, with the bishops and deacons:**
⁽²⁾ **Grace** *be* **unto you, and peace, from GOD our FATHER, and** *from* **the LORD JESUS CHRIST.**
⁽³⁾ **I thank my GOD upon every remembrance of you,**
⁽⁴⁾ **Always in every prayer of mine for you all making request with joy,**
⁽⁵⁾ **For your fellowship in the gospel from the first day until now;**
⁽⁶⁾ **Being confident of this very thing, that HE which hath begun a good work in you will perform** *it* **until the day of JESUS CHRIST:**
⁽⁷⁾ **Even as it is meet for me to think this of you all, because I have you in my heart; inasmuch as both in my bonds, and in the defence and confirmation of the gospel, ye all are partakers of my grace.**
⁽⁸⁾ **For GOD is my record, how greatly I long after you all in the bowels of JESUS CHRIST.**
⁽⁹⁾ **And this I pray, that your love may abound yet more and more in knowledge and** *in* **all judgment;**
⁽¹⁰⁾ **That ye may approve things that are excellent; that ye may be sincere and without offence till the day of CHRIST;**
⁽¹¹⁾ **Being filled with the fruits of righteousness, which are by JESUS CHRIST, unto the glory and praise of GOD.**

COMMENTARY:

Paul planted the Church at Philippi during his second missionary journey (Acts 16:11-40). Some years later he writes this letter to that church of believers whom he now identifies as "saints" equipped with bishops and deacons. He addresses this letter as being from himself and Timothy, his young protégé, and fellow servant of CHRIST JESUS.
Every time Paul thought of this, now fledgling church, he gave thanks to GOD, and prayed for them with joy in his heart for their dedication to the

work of CHRIST, spreading the Gospel, since they first heard it for themselves. He was confident that GOD would continue the great work that HE had begun in them, even up until the time that CHRIST JESUS returns and claims those whose hearts were filled with the things of GOD, and deny those, whose hearts remained fascinated with the things of this world.

In this passage, we see Paul stressing the ideology of "partnership among Christians". To be in CHRIST entails, not only, the idea of being "with CHRIST" in the Christian body, and sharing in HIS grace, but also, it means sharing in HIS work, and, in HIS suffering for the gospel.

www.ingramcontent.com/pod-product-compliance
Lightning Source LLC
Chambersburg PA
CBHW080448110426
42743CB00016B/3315